Over the past thirty years, Americans have rudely discovered that they had been taught what the writer Thomas Powers has called a 'child's history' of their government.

—Michael Beschloss
NEWSWEEK[1]

---

[1] NEWSWEEK, November 22, 1993, p. 62.

About the Uncle Eric Series

The Uncle Eric series of books is written by Richard J. Maybury for young and old alike. Using the epistolary style of writing (using letters to tell a story), Mr. Maybury plays the part of an economist writing a series of letters to his niece or nephew. Using stories and examples, he gives interesting and clear explanations of topics that are generally thought to be too difficult for anyone but experts.

Mr. Maybury warns, "beware of anyone who tells you a topic is above you or better left to experts. Many people are twice as smart as they think they are, but they've been intimidated into believing some topics are above them. You can understand almost anything if it is explained well."

The series is called UNCLE ERIC'S MODEL OF HOW THE WORLD WORKS. In the series, Mr. Maybury writes from the political, legal, and economic viewpoint of America's Founders. The books can be read in any order and have been written to stand alone. To get the most from each one, however, Mr. Maybury suggests the following order of reading:

Uncle Eric's Model
of How the World Works

An Uncle Eric Book

Are You Liberal? Conservative? or Confused?

Second Edition

by Richard J. Maybury
(Uncle Eric)

published by
Bluestocking Press
www.BluestockingPress.com

Printed and bound in the United States of America
Cover illustration by Bob O'Hara, Georgetown, CA
Cover design by Brian C. Williams, El Dorado, CA
Edited by Jane A. Williams

Library of Congress Cataloging-in-Publication Data

Maybury, Rick.
   Are you liberal? conservative? or confused? / by Richard J. Maybury
(Uncle Eric).-- 2nd ed.
      p. cm. -- (An Uncle Eric book)
   Includes bibliographical references and index.
   ISBN 0-942617-54-1 (soft cover : alk. paper)
   1. Political science--United States. 2. Ideology--United States.
   I. Title. II. Series.

   JA84.U5.M297 2004
   320.5 ' 0973--dc22   2004007718

   —

Published by Bluestocking Press • P.O. Box 1014
Placerville, CA 95667-1014
web site: www.BluestockingPress.com

To Bill Snavely,
whose encouragement
gave me the confidence
to keep trying.

Uncle Eric's Model of How the World Works

What is a model? In his book UNCLE ERIC TALKS ABOUT PERSONAL, CAREER, AND FINANCIAL SECURITY, Richard Maybury (Uncle Eric) explains that one of the most important things you can teach children or learn yourself is:

> Models are how we think, they are how we understand how the world works. As we go through life we build these very complex pictures in our minds of how the world works, and we're constantly referring back to them—matching incoming data against our models. That's how we make sense of things.
>
> One of the most important uses for models is in sorting incoming information to decide if it's important or not.
>
> In most schools, models are never mentioned because the teachers are unaware of them. One of the most dangerous weaknesses in traditional education is that it contains no model for political history. Teachers teach what they were taught—and no one ever mentioned models to them, so they don't teach them to their students.

For the most part, children are just loaded down with collections of facts that they are made to memorize. Without good models, children have no way to know which facts are important and which are not. Students leave school thinking history is a senseless waste of time. Then, deprived of the real lessons of history, the student is vulnerable.

The question is, which models to teach. Mr. Maybury says, "The two models that I think are crucially important for everyone to learn are economics and law."

WHATEVER HAPPENED TO PENNY CANDY? explains the economic model, which is based on Austrian economics, the most free-market of all economic models. WHATEVER HAPPENED TO JUSTICE? explains the legal model and shows the connection between rational law and economic progress. The legal model is the old British Common Law—or Natural Law. The original principles on which America was founded were those of the old British Common Law.

These two books, PENNY CANDY and JUSTICE, provide the overall model of how human civilization works, especially the world of money.

Once the model is understood, read ARE YOU LIBERAL? CONSERVATIVE? OR CONFUSED? This book explains political philosophies relative to Uncle Eric's Model—and makes a strong case for consistency to that model, no exceptions.

Next, read ANCIENT ROME: HOW IT AFFECTS YOU TODAY, which shows what happens when a society ignores Uncle Eric's Model and embraces fascism—an all too common practice these days, although the word fascism is never used.

To help you locate books and authors generally in agreement with these economic and legal models, Mr. Maybury wrote EVALUATING BOOKS: WHAT WOULD THOMAS JEFFERSON THINK ABOUT THIS? This book provides guidelines for selecting books that are consistent with the principles of America's Founders. You can apply these guidelines to books, movies, news commentators, and current events—to any spoken or written medium.

Further expanding on the economic model, THE MONEY MYSTERY explains the hidden force affecting your career, business, and investments. Some economists refer to this force as velocity, others to money demand. Whichever term is used, it is one of the least understood forces affecting your life. Knowing about velocity and money demand not only gives you an understanding of history that few others have, it prepares you to understand and avoid pitfalls in your career, business, and investments. THE MONEY MYSTERY is the first sequel to WHATEVER HAPPENED TO PENNY CANDY? It provides essential background for getting the most from THE CLIPPER SHIP STRATEGY.

THE CLIPPER SHIP STRATEGY explains how government's interference in the economy affects business, careers, and investments. It's a practical nuts-and-bolts strategy for prospering in our turbulent economy. This book is the second sequel to WHATEVER HAPPENED TO PENNY CANDY? and should be read after THE MONEY MYSTERY.

THE THOUSAND YEAR WAR IN THE MIDEAST: HOW IT AFFECTS YOU TODAY explains how events on the other side of the world a thousand years ago can affect us more than events in our own hometowns today. In the last quarter of the 20th century, the Thousand Year War has been the cause of great shocks to the investment markets—the oil embargoes, the Iranian hostage crisis, the Iraq-Kuwait war, the Caucasus Wars over the Caspian Sea oil basin, and September 11, 2001—and it is likely to remain so for decades to come. Forewarned is forearmed. You must understand where this war is leading to manage your career, business, and investments.

The explosion of the battleship Maine in Havana Harbor in 1898 was the beginning of a chain reaction that eventually led to the destruction of the World Trade Center. In his two-part World War series Richard Maybury explains that an unbroken line leads directly from the Spanish-American War through World War I, World War II, the Korean and Vietnam Wars, the Iraq-Kuwait War, and the "War on Terror" that began September 11, 2001. Mr. Maybury explains the other side of the story, the side you are not likely to get anywhere else, in this two-part World War series: WORLD WAR I: THE REST OF THE STORY AND HOW IT AFFECTS YOU TODAY and WORLD WAR II: THE REST OF THE STORY AND HOW IT AFFECTS YOU TODAY.

Uncle Eric's Model
of How the World Works

These books can be read in any order and have been written to stand alone. But to get the most from each one, Mr. Maybury suggests the following order of reading:

Book 1. UNCLE ERIC TALKS ABOUT PERSONAL, CAREER, AND FINANCIAL SECURITY.
Uncle Eric's Model introduced. Models (or paradigms) are how people think; they are how we understand our world. To achieve success in our careers, investments, and every other part of our lives, we need sound models. These help us recognize and use the information that is important and bypass that which is not. In this book, Mr. Maybury introduces the model he has found most useful. These are explained in WHATEVER HAPPENED TO PENNY CANDY? WHATEVER HAPPENED TO JUSTICE? and THE CLIPPER SHIP STRATEGY.
(Study Guide available.)

Book 2.   **WHATEVER HAPPENED TO PENNY CANDY?** A FAST,
CLEAR, AND FUN EXPLANATION OF THE ECONOMICS YOU
NEED FOR SUCCESS IN YOUR CAREER, BUSINESS, AND
INVESTMENTS. The economic model explained. The
clearest and most interesting explanation of
economics around. Learn about investment
cycles, velocity, business cycles, recessions,
inflation, money demand, and more. Contains
"Beyond the Basics," which supplements the basic
ideas and is included for readers who choose to
tackle more challenging concepts. Recommended
by former U.S. Treasury Secretary William Simon
and many others. *(Study Guide available.)*

Book 3.   **WHATEVER HAPPENED TO JUSTICE?**
The legal model explained. Explores America's
legal heritage. Shows what is wrong with our legal
system and economy, and how to fix it. Discusses
the difference between higher law and man-made
law, and the connection between rational law and
economic prosperity. Introduces the Two Laws:
1) do all you have agreed to do, and 2) do not
encroach on other persons or their property.
(Study Guide available.)

Book 4.   **ARE YOU LIBERAL? CONSERVATIVE? OR CONFUSED?**
Political labels. What do they mean? Liberal,
conservative, left, right, democrat, republican,
moderate, socialist, libertarian, communist—what
are their economic policies, and what plans do their
promoters have for your money? Clear, concise
explanations. Facts and fallacies.
(Study Guide available.)

Book 5. ANCIENT ROME: HOW IT AFFECTS YOU TODAY.
This book explains what happens when a society ignores the model. Are we heading for fascism like ancient Rome? Mr. Maybury uses historical events to explain current events, including the wars in the former Soviet Empire, and the legal and economic problems of America today. With the turmoil in Russia and Russia's return to fascism, you must read this book to understand your future. History does repeat. *(Study Guide available.)*

Book 6. EVALUATING BOOKS: WHAT WOULD THOMAS JEFFERSON THINK ABOUT THIS?
Most books, magazines, and news stories are slanted against the principles of America's Founders. Often the writers are not aware of it, they simply write as they were taught. Learn how to identify the bias so you can make informed reading, listening, and viewing choices.

Book 7. THE MONEY MYSTERY: THE HIDDEN FORCE AFFECTING YOUR CAREER, BUSINESS, AND INVESTMENTS.
The first sequel to WHATEVER HAPPENED TO PENNY CANDY? Some economists refer to velocity, others to money demand. However it is seen, it is one of the least understood forces affecting our businesses, careers, and investments—it is the financial trigger. This book discusses precautions you should take and explains why Federal Reserve officials remain so afraid of inflation. THE MONEY MYSTERY prepares you to understand and avoid pitfalls in your career, business, and investments. *(Study Guide available.)*

Book 8.   THE CLIPPER SHIP STRATEGY: FOR SUCCESS IN YOUR
CAREER, BUSINESS, AND INVESTMENTS.

The second sequel to WHATEVER HAPPENED TO PENNY
CANDY? Conventional wisdom says that when the
government expands the money supply, the money
descends on the economy in a uniform blanket.
This is wrong. The money is injected into specific
locations causing hot spots or "cones" such as the
tech bubble of the 1990s. Mr. Maybury explains
his system for tracking and profiting from these
cones. Practical nuts-and-bolts strategy for
prospering in our turbulent economy.
(Study Guide available.)

Book 9.   THE THOUSAND YEAR WAR IN THE MIDEAST: HOW IT
AFFECTS YOU TODAY.

Mr. Maybury shows that events on the other side
of the world a thousand years ago can affect us
more than events in our hometowns today. This
book explains the ten-century battle the U.S. has
entered against the Islamic world. It predicted the
events that began unfolding on September 11,
2001. It helps you understand the thinking of the
Muslims in the Mideast, and why the coming oil
war will affect investment markets around the
globe. In the last three decades this war has been
the cause of great shocks to the economy and
investment markets, including the oil embargoes,
the Iranian hostage crisis, the Iraq-Kuwait war,
the Caucasus Wars over the Caspian Sea oil basin,
and the September 11th attack—and it is likely to
remain so for decades to come. Forewarned is
forearmed. To successfully manage your career,

business, and investments, you must understand this war. *(Contact Bluestocking Press regarding Study Guide availability.)*

Book 10. WORLD WAR I: THE REST OF THE STORY AND HOW IT AFFECTS YOU TODAY, 1870 TO 1935.
The explosion of the battleship Maine in Havana Harbor in 1898 was the beginning of a chain reaction that continues today. Mr. Maybury presents an idea-based explanation of the First World War. He focuses on the ideas and events that led to World War I, events during the war, and how they led to World War II. Includes the ten deadly ideas that lead to war. *(Contact Bluestocking Press regarding Study Guide availability.)*

Book 11. WORLD WAR II: THE REST OF THE STORY AND HOW IT AFFECTS YOU TODAY, 1935 TO SEPTEMBER 11, 2001.
An idea-based explanation of the war. Focuses on events in the Second World War and how our misunderstanding of this war led to America's subsequent wars, including the Korean and Vietnam Wars, the Iraq-Kuwait War, and the "War on Terror" that began September 11, 2001. *(Contact Bluestocking Press regarding Study Guide availability.)*

Note to Reader

Throughout each "Uncle Eric" book, whenever a word that appears in the glossary is introduced in the text, it is displayed in a **bold typeface.**

Quantity Discounts Available

The Uncle Eric books are available at special quantity discounts for bulk purchases to individuals, businesses, schools, libraries, and associations.

For terms and discount schedule contact:

Special Sales Department
Bluestocking Press
Phone: 800-959-8586
email: CustomerService@BluestockingPress.com
web site: www.BluestockingPress.com

Specify how books are to be distributed: for classrooms, or as gifts, premiums, fund raisers—or to be resold.

Study Guide Available

A BLUESTOCKING GUIDE:
POLITICAL PHILOSOPHIES

by Jane A. Williams

— based on Richard J. Maybury's book —
ARE YOU LIBERAL? CONSERVATIVE? OR CONFUSED?

A BLUESTOCKING GUIDE: POLITICAL PHILOSOPHIES is designed to enhance a student's understanding and re-
tention of the subject matter presented in the corre-
sponding primer: ARE YOU LIBERAL? CONSERVATIVE? OR
CONFUSED? This study guide includes comprehension
questions and answers (relating to specific chapters
within the primer), application questions (to guide the
student in applying the concepts learned to everyday
life), and a final exam. Also included are research and
essay assignments, as well as thought questions to fa-
cilitate student-instructor discussion. In some cases,
suggestions for further reading are listed.

Order from your favorite book store or direct from
the publisher: Bluestocking Press (see order information on last page of this book).

Study Guides
are available or forthcoming
for other Uncle Eric books.

Contents

Author's Disclosure

For reasons I do not understand, writers today are supposed to be objective. Few disclose the viewpoints or opinions they use to decide what information is important and what is not, or what shall be presented or omitted.

I do not adhere to this standard and make no pretense of being objective. I am biased in favor of liberty, free markets, and international neutrality and proud of it. So I disclose my viewpoint, which you will find explained in detail in my other books.[2]

For those who have not yet read these publications, I call my viewpoint Juris Naturalism (pronounced *jur*-es *nach*-e-re-liz-em, sometimes abbreviated JN) meaning the belief in a natural law that is higher than any government's law. Here are six quotes from America's Founders that help to describe this viewpoint:

> ...all men are created equal, that they are endowed by their Creator with certain unalienable rights.
> —Declaration of Independence, 1776

> The natural rights of the colonists are these: first, a right to life; second to liberty; third to property; together with the right to support and defend them in the best manner they can.
> —Samuel Adams, 1772

---

[2] See Richard Maybury's other Uncle Eric books (see pgs. 6-13), published by Bluestocking Press, phone: 800-959-8586, web site: www.BluestockingPress.com

It is strangely absurd to suppose that a million of human beings collected together are not under the same moral laws which bind each of them separately.
—Thomas Jefferson, 1816

A wise and frugal government, which shall restrain men from injuring one another, which shall leave them otherwise free to regulate their own pursuits of industry and improvement, and shall not take from the mouth of labor the bread it has earned. This is the sum of good government.
—Thomas Jefferson, 1801

Not a place on earth might be so happy as America. Her situation is remote from all the wrangling world, and she has nothing to do but to trade with them.
—Thomas Paine, 1776

The great rule of conduct for us, in regard to foreign nations, is, in extending our commercial relations, to have with them as little political connection as possible.
—George Washington, 1796

George
Washington

 **1**

Don't Be Embarrassed

Dear Chris,

It's good to hear from you again. You wrote that your instructor has created a unit of study to help students become responsible citizens and voters. But you are confused by all the political labels: **liberal, conservative, left, right, democrat, republican, moderate, socialist, communist, fascist, libertarian, centrist, populist, green.**

You asked me to help you understand them. Specifically, you asked: "What do they mean? What are their economic and legal policies? What plans do these people have for my money? What model[3] do they follow?"

You said you're embarrassed that you don't know. Don't be. You might be surprised at the number of well-educated adults who have only a foggy notion of what these labels mean; they, too, are reluctant to admit it. This is one of those strange cases in which everyone assumes everyone else knows; they think it's common knowledge so no one ever bothers to ask or explain.

---

[3] For a discussion of models, see pages 6-13 of this book.

We'll start with a look at the left-and-right, or liberal-and-conservative, political spectrum and descriptions of each label. Then we'll look at the effects on the economy and our businesses, careers, and investments.

Chris, bear in mind that this will be only one man's opinion—mine. Political labels are a fuzzy subject, we have very few tight definitions, and I will be giving it to you the way I see it.

Before I begin, I'll give you my usual "truth in advertising" disclosure: this presentation will not be objective. Let me explain.

Suppose you are accused of a crime. And, suppose that during your trial you are not allowed to have a defense attorney, just a prosecuting attorney who promises to do a good job of presenting both sides of the story in an unbiased fashion. Would you feel you were getting a fair trial? Would the judge and jury be able to discover the truth?

In other words, why do American courts use defense attorneys as well as prosecuting attorneys? Why not do what many dictatorships do, save time and money by having only a prosecuting attorney who promises to be objective?

Because the prosecutor will not be—cannot be—objective.

Our courts are based on the assumption that truth is best discovered by listening to a debate between advocates. Each advocate does his best to present his side of the story and to show the weaknesses in the opposing side. This is a very old, tried and true principle of **common law**.

Most people today believe writers, especially journalists, should be objective. But true objectivity is as unlikely for a writer as it is for a court that has only a prosecuting attorney.

Before a writer sits down to write he must do research. He must collect a set of facts about the topic. If the research is thorough, the collection of facts will be far greater than will fit into the article or book. To decide which facts to present, the writer must separate those that are more important from those that are less important.

That's the problem. How does the writer decide what's important?

It depends on the writer's viewpoint—on the writer's model, or idea, of how the world works, and on the writer's sense of right and wrong. This is all opinion.

In the so-called **hard sciences** such as physics and chemistry, truth can be scientifically proven. But in most other subjects, proof is elusive, and even expert opinion is, at bottom, still opinion; experts have often been wrong.

So, the writer selects what's important on the basis of his or her own opinion. There is no other way.

This leaves the writer in a quandary: how to appear objective, as everyone says a writer should be, when objectivity is not possible.

In the mainstream press most writers resort to using the left-and-right political spectrum. They try to give "both sides of the story," meaning two sets of facts and analysis, one set acceptable to the left and the other acceptable to the right. This passes for objectivity and it's probably the best the writers can do under the circumstances, but it is wrong on three points.

First, the range of viewpoints is much greater and more diverse than the simple left-and-right political spectrum. I will explain this in detail in future letters.

Second, the writer is human. He has his own set of opinions and is more skilled at presenting these than at presenting opinions of others. No matter how hard he tries, his "objective" presentation is likely to be unintentionally slanted.

Third, the forced use of the left-and-right spectrum has led to oversimplification. Many people now assume there is just left and right, nothing else, and they think all political viewpoints are just shades of one side or the other. This is quite wrong, as I'll explain later.

These three barriers to objectivity permeate not only television and radio news reports but magazine articles, newspapers, school books, and more—anything that deals with public issues. Chris, from this moment on you can test this yourself by noting how frequently this left-right spectrum is used to the exclusion of all other viewpoints.

I try to avoid the objectivity trap by freely disclosing my viewpoint. My readers know exactly what they're getting from me and, aware of my slant, they can go in search of other viewpoints to balance against mine. Chris, I believe this is the only way a reader can fairly judge and understand any topic outside the hard sciences. If he goes in search of "objective" articles and books, he will end up being misled.

Since you've read my previous sets of letters about economics, law, and government[4] you already know my viewpoint. It's an endangered viewpoint today, and the main reason I write you these letters is to make sure you hear it.

---

[4] When Mr. Maybury refers to "his previous letters" he is referring to the other "Uncle Eric" books mentioned on pages 7 and 8 of this book. Each "Uncle Eric" book builds on the information in others. Each can be read independently of the others, but readers will get the most from each one by reading the entire series in the recommended order. In this particular instance he is referring to WHATEVER HAPPENED TO PENNY CANDY? and WHATEVER HAPPENED TO JUSTICE?

As I've said many times before, Chris, if you don't get this side of the story from me you'll probably never get it anywhere. It has been nearly erased from American culture. To find it you need to go back to the original writings of America's Founders, or to the writings of the very few persons today who have a deep understanding of the political, economic, and historical beliefs of the Founders.

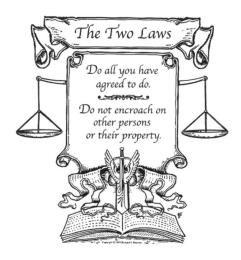

The Two Laws

Do all you have agreed to do.

Do not encroach on other persons or their property.

Other than referring to my viewpoint as the original American philosophy I've never found it necessary to coin a label. It's appropriate now, however, because I'm writing to you about political labels. I need a little time to do some research, to make sure I find a word or words that best describes my viewpoint. Until then remember, *if it isn't math, physics, chemistry, or biology, it's an **editorial**.* Read it with a critical eye, and that goes for my work as well as everyone else's. No one is infallible.

Uncle Eric

2

The Original
American Philosophy

Dear Chris,

I have finally come up with a label to describe the original American philosophy, which is also my viewpoint. Before I tell you the name, however, I'd like to provide you with some historical background.

Over the centuries the viewpoint you found in my previous letters has had several labels. The original label was "classical liberalism." Thomas Jefferson, Patrick Henry, James Madison, and the other American Founders were classical liberals. A more recent name for the original American philosophy is "libertarianism."

I do not like either of them. They are often misused by persons who do not understand them, so they can be misleading. And they are too similar to other, more well-known labels which refer to something quite different than the original American philosophy. **Classical liberal** sounds too much like "liberal," which is something vastly different. "Libertarian" sounds too much like **civil libertarian**, also something vastly different.

By the way, Chris, misuse is a problem with all labels. We need words to communicate, but misuse of words will foster miscommunication, followed by misunderstanding. A good rule whenever you're in a conversation or debate with someone is to ask the individual to define the label or key word under discussion, or any other word that is subject to slant or bias.

In my research I came up with a term that describes the original American philosophy, but is obscure today. The term is rarely used, so it is rarely misused. It is **juris naturalis** (pronounced *jur*-es *nach*-e-re-liz).[5] This is Latin for **Natural[6] Law**. Natural Law is also called **Higher Law** and was explained in detail in my previous set of letters. I'll summarize here.

Higher Law is the belief that right and wrong are not matters of opinion. Like the laws of physics, chemistry, and biology, right and wrong are a given, something that we must learn and apply. They cannot be made up by politicians or anyone else. They are part of what humans are, our Creator gave them to us. They have been built into our DNA.[7]

When obedience to Higher Law is widespread, life gets better. When it's not, life gets worse.

---

[5] It can also be jus naturale.

[6] The fact that a political group may have the words "natural law" in its name does not mean it necessarily has any interest in the type of Natural Law explained in this book. One test is to check the party platform to see if they want to protect your rights to your property.

[7] Our Creator built Higher Law into our DNA in the same sense as our DNA contains the instructions for our emotions, minds, skills, and talents. The way we choose to use them is up to us. A pro quarterback has a talent for throwing a football, but his use of the talent is his choice.

Higher Law is above any government's **law**, and when a government violates Higher Law, life for most of society gets worse.

What specifically are the Higher Laws? Two are common to all major religions and philosophies. The first is, do all you have agreed to do. This is the basis of **contract law**.

The second is, do not **encroach** on other persons or their property. This is the basis of **tort law** and some **criminal law** (laws against theft, assault, kidnapping, etc.). The American Founders wanted a government that would, above all, keep its encroachments extremely limited.

Being common to all major religions and philosophies, these two laws were the basis of the old common law, and common law was the origin of the American system of liberty. For thousands of years they have been revered and enforced by courts around the world because they have been found to work.

Found is an important word here. Higher Law is discovered law. In courts where Higher Law is enforced, the question always before the judge and jury is, what is justice and how do we apply it? They are trying to find it, not make it up.

Let me emphasize that a fundamental principle in Higher Law is that a government cannot make up laws of human conduct any more than it can make up laws of physics, chemistry, or biology. A government that tries to make up law is playing God.

The term I'll coin for a person who believes in the supremacy of Higher Law, or Natural Law, is a **juris naturalist**. He believes in **juris naturalism**. He is convinced government should obey Higher Law just as everyone else should. Government should not encroach on persons who have not harmed anyone.

This means a juris naturalist wants to minimize **political power** and government. Why? Because political power is the privilege of using force on persons who have not harmed anyone. It is the privilege of encroachment. This is the characteristic that makes **government** — a government. No other institution has this privilege.

> **Political Power**
>
> The characteristic that sets government apart from all other institutions. The privilege of using force on persons who have not harmed anyone.

And, no human can encroach on someone who has not harmed anyone without being corrupted.

So, the juris naturalist believes political power is fundamentally evil, it corrupts. Key point: political power corrupts not only the morals but also the judgment.

Let me say here, Chris, that many people go into politics with the admirable goal of fighting corruption. But if a good person were put in charge of the Mafia, would the Mafia be cleaned up or would the good person be corrupted? History gives the answer over and over.

You can conduct your own research on this. Study U.S. politicians from 1787. Even America's Founders, who were so aware of the dangers of political power, when given that political power, abused it. Read about John Adams. He was a most uncompromising statesman and politician. He retired from politics to avoid being corrupted by power.

By the way, Chris, I am aware that many ancient books from around the world say man needs government, or even that government is the work of a deity. I wonder how many of these cases are mistranslations—cases where the original writer, using a nearly forgotten language, wrote the writer's word for "law", but in later centuries scribes using other languages mistranslated the word "law" and wrote "government".

Over the centuries, the meanings of many words have been changed to the point that confusion reigns. Today people use the words government and **state** interchangeably with law, so the distinction has been lost, especially in the translation of ancient books about law and government.

Recognizing the danger of political power, the juris naturalist wants to continually reduce government until someday it disappears entirely—government, that is, *not law*. They are not the same thing. That day may be far in the future, but the juris naturalist believes we must be always consciously headed in that direction in order to avoid going in the other direction, toward more government.

The juris naturalist sees the complete absence of government as a kind of ideal, an eventual goal, and wants to move toward it. Realistically, however, he doubts we'll get there any time soon, if ever, because most of the world still believes large, powerful governments are necessary. If a government were eliminated, someone would just come along and set up a new one.

In other words, the juris naturalist argues that the choice of no government simply does not exist. There *will* be a government. The best we can do at this time is minimize it, which is what America's Founders were trying to do.

Another way to look at it, says the juris naturalist, is that political power is like **crime**. It cannot be totally eradicated, but because it is evil we should work constantly to reduce it as much as possible. And just because it is inevitable does not

mean we should embrace it as a solution to our problems. Even if crime is used with good intentions, it remains evil, as does political power.

This brings up another important point that we discussed in our previous letters and I want to emphasize here. As I said before, law and government are not the same thing.

Every rational person wants law, especially the two fundamental laws: 1) do all you have agreed to do, and 2) do not encroach on other persons or their property. These seventeen words are what make civilization possible.

But government (or the state) is something different. In fact, we can make a strong case that government is the opposite of law—even that some governments were invented to destroy law because government is the only institution that claims the legal privilege of encroaching on persons who have not harmed anyone. This is what it was in the beginning and this is what it remains today—the institution that claims the right to violate the two fundamental laws.

Chris, we've discussed these ideas before. In 1750, in the years prior to the American Revolution, an American colonist and clergyman, Jonathan Mayhew, challenged his congregation to choose between Higher Law and government's law.[8] The citizenry could not have both because the English government, Mayhew believed, was violating Higher Law.

Think about it, Chris. If everyone lived by the two fundamental laws, would government be necessary? Has anyone ever suggested to you that government may not be necessary?

Is law necessary? Yes. Government? I wonder.

---

[8] See JONATHAN MAYHEW'S SERMON published by Bluestocking Press, web site: www.BluestockingPress.com

The institution of government reminds me of the institution of slavery. Imagine going back to 18th century America and arguing that slavery was not necessary. People would have called you crazy, their reaction would have been something like this:

Get rid of slavery? You're insane. Mankind has had slavery since the beginning of history. It's a necessity, nearly every culture has it or has had it at one time or another.

If we had no slaves, who would chop the firewood to keep us warm in winter? Who would grow the cotton and corn? Who would feed the chickens? Who would make our clothing?

Get rid of slavery? We'd freeze. We'd starve. In a year's time we'd all be dead.

But slavery in America is gone now, and we don't freeze, and we don't starve. In fact, the typical American today lives far better than any slave owner ever did. We all know that the arguments in favor of slavery were wrong both morally and practically. It wasn't so clear 200 years ago but it is today. The arguments for the necessity of slavery were propaganda.

Today, millions benefit from the government's privilege of encroaching, so we've all been taught to believe law and government are the same thing, and since law is necessary we assume government is, too.

But, again, this is not to say government isn't inevitable. The American Founders understood this. They knew that government was, and probably always would be, popular, and if they didn't set one up someone else would. The choice of having no government did not exist then, nor does it today.

In fact, Chris, in the 21st century people appear to be more desirous of large, powerful governments than at any time since the Roman Empire. Because there is such an overwhelming demand for the state, there will be a supply, it is inevitable.

This is the premise of all political philosophies today: there *will* be a state, so what kind will it be?

The juris naturalist wants the smallest, weakest one possible. He knows his desire for a world without political power may forever remain unfulfilled, but he uses it as his guiding star. Whenever he strays in the direction of more government, for whatever reason, his alarm bells ring. The juris naturalist believes the most important question for public debate is, "How can we get this or that essential service without it being done by government?"

A juris naturalist believes government should be used to solve problems only in cases where the benefits are clearly greater than the costs. This means *all* costs, hidden as well as visible.

Another key point: the juris naturalist may not be able to prove it, but he strongly suspects that in all cases of government activity the total costs to all persons affected are greater than total benefits.

The juris naturalist wants problems solved through private means, especially through free markets and free enterprise. If you've gotten into the recommended reading in my previous sets of letters you know how this can work.

How would a juris naturalist reduce government? Here's one idea I'll modestly call the Uncle Eric Plan.

Everyone believes government has enacted too many laws and wastes too much money. You will find no rational person on this planet who would disagree with that. We have thousands of unnecessary laws and billions of dollars of unnecessary spending, and everyone knows it.

Note that all government spending occurs under order of some law.

Under the Uncle Eric Plan, we'd have a constitutional amendment saying lawmakers could not make any new law unless, at the same time, they repealed five.

Would the Uncle Eric Plan have a realistic chance of enactment? If it became popular, I believe so. It takes advantage of the political structure's greatest weakness, shortsightedness. Governments do little real long-term planning. Anything that's more than a few months in the future is considered too far away to worry about.

We have thousands of old, outdated laws. For a year or two after the Uncle Eric Plan is enacted lawmakers will have no trouble finding insignificant laws to repeal. The plan won't begin to bite until after the next election, and in Washington the attitude is always, "We'll cross that bridge when we come to it."

Returning to the question of political labels, if a person who wants a small, weak government is a juris naturalist, what do you think we call someone who wants a large, powerful government?

Next letter.

Uncle Eric

3

The Opposite of the
Original American Philosophy

Dear Chris,

You're right. The opposite of a juris naturalist is a **statist**. I see you are recalling information from our prior sets of letters. A statist believes government *can* perform services in which benefits are greater than total costs.

The juris naturalist asks, where is the evidence for this?

The statist rarely has evidence, or at least rarely has any, that can stand up under close scrutiny. The hidden costs of government are legion.

To a juris naturalist, the statist's belief that government can be, on balance, good, is a superstition. It is not supported by evidence.

In every case I've ever seen, when all the hidden costs of a government activity are uncovered, they are greater than the benefits.

But my experience has also been that almost every source of information we are exposed to today—newspapers, radio, TV, movies, schoolbooks and even church literature — has a statist slant. **Statism** has become America's national religion. It sometimes seems that "more laws, more taxes, and more law enforcement" has become the answer to every problem.

Chris, name any issue you are concerned about—drug addiction, poverty, illiteracy, bigotry, pollution, whatever— and you'll see little attempt to do anything about the root cause. There is only a demand for more government. This, in most cases, is really a demand for more of the cause.

In my letters I try to give you the other side of the story, the juris naturalist side, because the fundamental principles of America's Founders have been almost totally erased from our culture. Today, almost all viewpoints are statist of one stripe or another. Here's why.

How many pages would a history book need to be in order to present all viewpoints? Such a book would be so long that few, if any, would buy it or read it. Obviously, a publisher has little incentive to publish what can't be sold.

So, even if writers would like to explain why a given political law or policy was enacted and give us all the various viewpoints and arguments, pro and con, they can't. Writers are forced to give only the reasons why the law or policy was passed—the pro arguments. Most con arguments, which include the arguments for liberty and free markets, are lost. History books automatically acquire a statist slant.

Incidentally, speaking of hidden costs, here's a good research project for you. Pick any government program you believe is unquestionably good and try to uncover all the hidden costs. Then match the hidden and unhidden costs against all the benefits, and see if you still think the benefits are greater than the costs.

For instance, suppose a company in your town is being subsidized because it is losing money and in danger of going out of business. It employs 1,000 workers who would lose their jobs without the government's help. Is this a good program?

On the surface, yes, but look deeper. The subsidy is paid for by taxpayers. Each dollar taxpayers pour into that company is a dollar they don't have to spend on shoes, television sets, cars, or whatever else they would otherwise buy. The firms who sell these shoes, television sets, etc., are unable to sell as much, so they need fewer workers. Jobs protected in your town are offset by jobs lost elsewhere. But these lost jobs are not noticed because they are scattered all over the country. The protected jobs are concentrated in a single easy-to-identify location.

This can also be a good debating technique. If someone advocates a government program, ask, "What are the hidden costs of this program?"

"Hidden costs? What do you mean hidden costs? There are no hidden costs."

"Come now, a go*vernment* program with *no* hidden costs? Surely you jest."

Then invite them to join you in discussing the possible hidden costs. In a polite and friendly and highly persuasive fashion, you'll lead them into defeating their own argument.

Interestingly, after everything I've said about objectivity being impossible, I do believe a juris naturalist can, in a sense, be objective about the dominant viewpoints: the liberals, moderates, and conservatives. The juris naturalist is an outsider, he strongly disagrees with all of them because they are all statist. So, he can be fair in showing how they differ from each other. He may have a hard time being unbiased in how statists differ from him, but not how they differ among themselves.

So, Chris, bear in mind that as you read these explanations of political labels, you are getting them from an outsider's, a juris naturalist's, viewpoint.

In my next letter we'll look at the basic political spectrum.

Uncle Eric

The American Founders were Juris Naturalists

4

Basic Political Spectrum

Dear Chris,

As commonly used today, here is the left-right political spectrum.

Left-Right Political Spectrum

As the words are generally used, **left** means liberal, and **right** means conservative.

Legend has it that this spectrum came from the 1789 French National Assembly in which the liberals were grouped on the left of the presiding officer and the conservatives on the right.

The labels refer to the temperament of the individual as well as the policies he or she favors. The meanings of some labels have changed over time. Presently liberal and conservative refer to these temperaments:

> **LIBERAL**. According to the COLUMBIA ENCYCLOPEDIA Third Edition, liberalism "is based, in general, on faith in progress and in the ability and goodness of man, and on firm belief in the importance of the rights and welfare of the individual." Also, "liberalism advocates steady change."

> **CONSERVATIVE,** says the same source, is "the desire to maintain, or conserve, the existing order. Conservatives value highly the wisdom of the past and are generally opposed to widespread reform."

Liberals tend to emphasize caring, gentleness, and progress. Conservatives tend to emphasize ruggedness, endurance, and stability. During the Vietnam War, liberals were "doves," their objective was peace; conservatives were "hawks," their objective was victory.

Remember, Chris, we are speaking here of temperaments, not specific policies.

The policies advocated by left and right can appear complex, but they are easily understood if we focus on the central issue, political power. This power is the prize the left and right compete to control. They disagree about the proper uses of it.

In my next letter we'll examine this power, then the liberal and conservative views on its use.

Uncle Eric

5

The Nature of Political Power

Dear Chris,

In past centuries the word power usually meant political power. When Lord Acton said power corrupts, everyone knew he was speaking of political power.

Today the word power is more broadly used. We speak of computer power, hydroelectric power, economic power, atomic power, and so on. Many activists use the words "power" and "**influence**" interchangeably, this adds to the confusion.

Political power is a special kind of power and it differs greatly from influence. As mentioned in an earlier letter, political power is the essence of government.

What is government? What sets it apart from all other human institutions?

We covered that in my previous set of letters. Here's a quick recap:

Governments are not institutions with superhuman abilities, they are organizations comprised of ordinary people. Like the rest of us, these people have needs, wants, desires, homes, families, loves, hates, quarrels, and vices.

The only characteristic that sets these humans apart from those who run businesses, charities, and other "private" institutions is that they have the privilege of using brute force to back up their decisions. This is political power. It is the privilege of telling others, "Do as we say or we will send people with guns to haul you away to prison." The people with guns are the police and military.

No other institution can do this. General Motors, the Presbyterian Church, or the Red Cross cannot tell you to purchase their services or be carried off to prison. Only government can force you to buy what it is selling. This is called taxation, and it is the political power most often used on us.

It's also the one people most often rebel against. On March 22, 1775, Edmund Burke tried to explain to the **House of Commons** why the American colonists were angry:

> The fierce spirit of Liberty is stronger in the English Colonies probably than in any other people on earth . . . They are therefore not only devoted to Liberty, but to Liberty according to English ideas, and on English principles . . . It happened, you know, Sir, that the great contests for freedom in this country were from the earliest times chiefly upon the question of Taxing.[9]

A few of the many other applications of political power are military conscription, laws against drug use, and gun ownership, and laws requiring all workers to participate in the Social Security system. Each uses force or threats of force to induce our obedience. Conservatives generally support military conscription and laws against drug use. Liberals generally support laws against guns and laws forcing your participation in Social Security.

---

[9] FOR GOOD AND EVIL by Charles Adams, Madison Books, Lanham, MD, 1993, p. 383.

Political power is brute force, this is what sets it apart from influence. Influence implies choice, you can choose to walk away.

As explained in my previous letters, a basic principle taught by all religions and philosophies is, do not encroach on other persons or their property. The religions and philosophies express this principle in different ways. Christians derive the principle from the Bible and use different words than Muslims, Jews, Hindus and others, but this principle is the foundation of every culture's rules against assault, kidnapping, and theft. Thou shalt not kill. Thou shalt not steal. Do not encroach.

Government is the one and only institution with the privilege of violating this principle. Governments encroach, this is what they were invented to do, which is why America's Founders believed government is an inherently evil institution. Thomas Paine said, "Government, even in its best state, is but a necessary evil."

Businesses, charities, and other "private" institutions can use verbal persuasion, peer pressure, offers of money, or other means to induce you to behave as they wish—they can use influence—but they are not allowed to use brute force; you can always walk away. With government you cannot walk away. Officials have the privilege of sending people with guns to your home to force you to obey their wishes.

Both conservatives and liberals—left and right—want this privilege. They disagree only in the specific applications of it.

In my next letter we'll cover the two general categories of encroachment.

Uncle Eric

6

The Two Categories
of Encroachment

Dear Chris,

As statism becomes more prevalent, so does encroachment. Liberals and conservatives both agree that encroaching on you is a fine and necessary thing. They disagree only over the specific details, which can be placed in two categories, "economic" and "social."

In the 1990s, many liberals adopted conservative ideas about economics. This causes the distinctions to become more muddled. But for now, to avoid confusion, I'll define the strict liberal and conservative agendas, without any shades of gray.

Let me emphasize that these are generalizations. Few people who regard themselves as liberal or conservative will be so 100%, most will have a few exceptions. Most liberals agree with conservatives to some extent, and most conservatives agree with liberals to some extent.

As I said, liberals and conservatives both agree that encroaching on you is a fine and necessary thing; they disagree only on the details. These are economic and social.

Economic refers to your money, work, career, production, trade, investments, and such. In these matters, liberals willingly encroach on you but conservatives believe you should remain largely free.

Social refers to virtually everything else: alcohol, tobacco and other drugs you might use, books and magazines you read, movies you watch, gambling, sexual practices, and the four-letter words you might say. In these matters conservatives wish to control you but liberals will allow you to remain largely free.

Another way of looking at the left-right disagreement is to focus on privacy. Liberals believe you should have privacy in your social conduct but not in your economic conduct. Conservatives grant privacy in your economic conduct but not in your social conduct.

Still another way to look at left and right is that the right wants to use force to stamp out **immorality**.[10] The left wants to use it to stamp out inequality of **wealth**.

Chris, here is an important point. Liberals are juris naturalists in social matters, but they tend to be statists in economic matters. Conservatives are the opposite, juris naturalists in economic matters and statists in social matters.

---

[10] The word immorality is not tightly defined, so if a person wants to use law (force) to stamp out immorality, we must ask what he or she means. Immorality is almost always accepted to mean extra-marital sex, but beyond that, there is much disagreement. Does it also mean drinking, or just drunkenness? Gambling? Use of heroin and cocaine? Marijuana? Tobacco? Caffeine? A further difficulty with the word is that "moral" is from the Latin "mores," meaning custom. To do what is immoral is to do what is not customary; if the majority change their opinion about what is right and wrong, then right and wrong change. By contrast, the word ethics is from the Latin "ethica," which refers to a set of rules of right and wrong that exist apart from opinion.

This can lead to confusion. If you hear a liberal speaking about social matters, you might jump to the conclusion that he or she is a juris naturalist. Similarly, if you hear a conservative talk about economics, you might think he or she is a juris naturalist.

When you are trying to discover a person's political beliefs, listen for opinions on a wide range of issues.

Let me make two points here to avert possible misunderstandings. First, none of this is meant to imply that juris naturalists are in favor of poverty, drug addiction, child pornography, or any other evils. It means only that the juris naturalist favors the non-government ways of solving these problems, the voluntary ways, and he is convinced that when government gets involved it only makes things worse.

Second, none of what I'm saying in this series of letters or anywhere else is meant to imply that liberals or conservatives are bad people or that they have bad intentions. In most cases I'm certain these people participate in the scramble for power simply because they do not know there is another way. The system of liberty described in my previous sets of letters has been forgotten, so the whole world, including the United States, is locked into a mode of dominate or be dominated.

Chris, political power corrupts everything it touches. How can political power not corrupt, when it is itself corruption? Remember the definition of political power: it is the privilege of encroaching on persons who have not harmed anyone. What human could exercise this privilege without having his sense of right and wrong corroded away?

In my next letter we'll look at the beliefs and policies of moderates.

Uncle Eric

Issue	Juris Naturalist (Wants Liberty)	Statist (Wants Encroachment)
Gun Control		
Liberal		*
Conservative	*	
Taxes for Welfare		
Liberal		*
Conservative	*	
Drug Use		
Liberal	*	
Conservative		*
Pornography		
Liberal	*	
Conservative		*
Wage & Price Controls		
Liberal		*
Conservative	*	
Socialized Medicine		
Liberal		*
Conservative	*	
Sexual Preference		
Liberal	*	
Conservative		*
Labor Unions		
Liberal		*
Conservative	*	
Prostitution		
Liberal	*	
Conservative		*

7

The Middle Ground

Dear Chris,

Midway between left and right is the **moderate** position, which is a combination of the other two. Moderates are sometimes called **centrists**, meaning they are in the center, which many people find comfortable because it is not near the "extremes" of left or right.

A moderate compromises. Borrowing from both left and right, he wishes to control both your economic conduct and your social conduct.

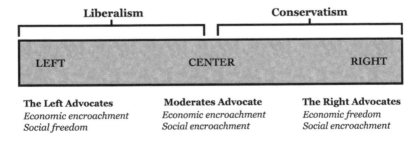

The Left Advocates	Moderates Advocate	The Right Advocates
Economic encroachment	*Economic encroachment*	*Economic freedom*
Social freedom	*Social encroachment*	*Social encroachment*

The moderate generally doesn't want to be as strict as left or right, but he wants to control both areas of your life. This means, among other things, that the total amount of power he wishes to hold over you is equal to or greater than that desired by either left or right.

An important but often overlooked point about moderates concerns privacy. Moderates will allow you more economic freedom than liberals and more social freedom than conservatives but they want to keep a close eye on both areas. They don't like privacy. They want to be able to monitor all your conduct so that they can clamp down on you whenever they think you've gone too far to either extreme.

In other words, as long as you don't force your behavior onto others, liberals generally couldn't care less what you read, say, or insert in your body. Conservatives couldn't care less how you work, invest, save, or spend. Moderates care about all of it, and they want to keep a close eye on all of it.

In the next letter I'll write a bit about freedom versus liberty.

Uncle Eric

8

Freedom vs. Liberty

Dear Chris,

Talking about liberals, moderates, and conservatives, brings up an important issue, the difference between **freedom** and **liberty**.

Freedom is a weak word, it can mean that you have an inalienable[11] right to do something, but it can also mean you have only *permission* to do it. Permission is necessarily granted by someone, which means freedom can be revoked by that someone. This is not the same as liberty.

Liberty was described by Thomas Jefferson in the Declaration of Independence when he wrote "all men are endowed by their Creator" with certain rights. Liberty is a right endowed by the Creator. It is a part of you, like your mind and emotions, it cannot be revoked.

Freedom is tenuous, but liberty cannot be rightfully violated by anyone except the Creator or the individual who owns the liberty.

---

[11] For an excellent discussion of inalienable rights see COMMON SENSE and THE DECLARATION OF INDEPENDENCE audio history produced by Knowledge Products, Nashville, TN, narrated by Craig Deitschmann (or search the web for this product).

If an individual encroaches on others, he has made an explicit decision to place himself outside the laws of civilization. It was his choice, no one else's. Under the system of liberty, this is the *only* case in which an individual's rights can be violated — at the individual's own choice.

Under freedom, others can negate an individual's rights any time they can acquire enough political power to do so. It is called majority rule. As you recall from our previous sets of letters, America's Founders did not like democracy and did not trust it. They wanted liberty.

*Liberty
Enlightening the World*

Although the word liberty is still heard today, few people acknowledge its existence in actual practice. Most acknowledge only freedom, which they seek to control. They want the privilege of deciding where you will be free and where you won't. They want to encroach on you in whatever areas of your life they deem necessary, and they hope to persuade the majority to agree to this.

Unfortunately, English, like all other languages, has limitations. Sometimes the word freedom is the best word for a particular sentence. So, when you see that word, Chris, read it with caution, and remember its weaknesses.

In my next letter we'll talk about exceptions.

Uncle Eric

9

Exceptions

Dear Chris,

Precision is difficult to achieve when dealing with political labels. We have no scientific tests to determine exactly where a person is on the political spectrum.

Also, each individual has personal exceptions. By temperament a person might be strongly liberal but willing to allow one or two exceptions that are far right. Or he might be conservative but willing to allow exceptions that are far left.

Governments, because they are comprised of people, behave inconsistently as well. A government might be strongly conservative or liberal, but it will contain hundreds of individuals of the opposite temperament working for changes. Here are some locations of nations on the political spectrum.

Example Nations

former U.S.S.R	Sweden	Britain	U.S.	Switzerland	Pinochet's Chile	Nazi Germany
LEFT			CENTER			RIGHT

Notice I've shown the U.S.S.R. — not Russia. This refers to the Union of Soviet Socialist Republics before 1990. In 1991 the Soviet Empire disintegrated and, in many areas, **socialism** has now been rejected. The people are still searching for a system they like, and this will probably go on for years, maybe decades.

Speaking of exceptions and the old U.S.S.R., which was a terrible dictatorship, this is a good spot to explain how liberty is so often lost. Most people feel deep in their hearts that liberty is a good thing, but they also have exceptions. For instance, as pointed out earlier, conservatives want you to have liberty in your business dealings but not in your social conduct; liberals are the opposite.

It is these exceptions that destroy liberty. Each person has a few pet exceptions. In a nation the size of the U.S., the exceptions number in the millions. As they are enacted into law, liberty is slowly destroyed.

This is the main reason a juris naturalist tends to sound so fanatical about protecting liberty. Once the door is opened to exceptions... well, you get the picture. By the way, Chris, you might compare the United States today with the United States of 1800. How many liberties have we lost? As you do the research, note the reasons — the good intentions — for each encroachment. A good place to start is with taxes. How many taxes and how burdensome were they in 1800? Today?

So far we have been talking about domestic issues. In my next letter we'll talk about the military and foreign policies of left and right.

Uncle Eric

10

Military and Foreign Policy

Dear Chris,

As I said, so far we have been talking about domestic issues — those that affect individuals in their own homelands. Liberals and conservatives also disagree about issues relating to the government's conduct toward other cultures and other governments — the so-called military and foreign policy.

This is now an area of great confusion.

Until the Soviet Empire collapsed, left and right had clear differences. Liberals did not want officials to form military alliances or intervene in the political affairs of other nations. They made one exception, economic assistance. Liberals were willing to raise taxes at home to finance aid to the poor abroad.

Conservatives were quite willing to form military alliances with other nations as long as officials of these nations claimed to be anti-Soviet. Conservatives were also willing to intervene in the affairs of other nations to keep these nations from drifting leftward. But they were cool toward the idea of sending money to help the poor. They believed that aid to the poor was often wasted or siphoned off to fill the pockets of corrupt officials. Conservatives tended to believe, however, that military aid was less subject to such abuse.

Now, with the Soviet Empire out of business, neither the left nor the right have a clear idea of their foreign policies. If, for instance, a foreign intervention is claimed to be a "humanitarian" mission to help the starving or the oppressed, some liberals and conservatives will support it, but others won't.

There isn't much else to say about this until left and right sort out their differences, which could take decades.

Chris, are you curious about the juris naturalist view on military and foreign policy? It hasn't changed, but it has been almost forgotten. As I said in an earlier letter, if you don't hear the juris naturalist view from me you'll probably never hear it at all unless you read the writings of America's Founders. George Washington had a lot to say about this. I'll enclose an excerpt from WASHINGTON'S FAREWELL ADDRESS.

The juris naturalist has always advised against foreign intervention of any kind, be it economic or military; he wants neutrality. The juris naturalist says we can never fully understand why other cultures behave as they do—we have a hard enough time understanding ourselves—and if we stick our noses into other people's business we inevitably get drawn into their wars. Examples are the two world wars, Vietnam, Korea, the 1990-91 Iraq-Kuwait War, the War on Terror. . . the list goes on and on.

This is not an argument for so-called isolationism. The juris naturalist likes to see Americans traveling, doing business abroad, and making friends there. But he wants no political connections. Americans, notes the juris naturalist, are probably the only persons on earth who think they are entitled to visit other nations secure in the knowledge that if they get into trouble the Marines will be sent to rescue them. This never was true except in a limited sense. It was mostly an illusion, but, in cases where it was true, it should end. If you travel or do business abroad, says the juris naturalist, you should do so at your own risk, as everyone else in the world does. If you don't like the risks, don't go. The world is, and always has been, a dangerous place. The lives of American troops should not be spent rescuing you from a situation you entered voluntarily.

I should point out here that the Constitution contains a major flaw in regard to foreign policy. The Bill of Rights stops at the border. The United States government's behavior toward you and me is severely restricted by the Bill of Rights, but to people in other nations the government can legally do almost anything it pleases. In the name of fighting communism, for instance, United States officials supported some of the most ruthless dictators on earth, including the Shah of Iran, Batista in Cuba, Marcos in the Philippines, Mobutu in Zaire, and even Saddam Hussein in Iraq. These thugs tortured, terrorized, and murdered thousands of their people, and today millions of their people still hate us. If U.S. officials had participated in this brutality inside the U.S., the least punishment they would have received would have been life imprisonment. Note that politicians of both the left and right have done this.

In my next letter we will take a look at republicans and democrats.

Uncle Eric

Washington's Farewell Address

Excerpt

Nothing is more essential than that permanent, inveterate antipathies against particular nations, and passionate attachments for others, should be excluded; and that, in place of them, just and amicable feelings towards all should be cultivated. The nation which indulges towards another an habitual hatred, or an habitual fondness, is in some degree a slave. It is a slave to its animosity or to its affections, either of which is sufficient to lead it astray from its duty and its interest. Antipathy in one nation against another disposes each more readily to offer insult and injury, to lay hold of slight causes of umbrage, and to be haughty and intractable when accidental or trifling occasions of dispute occur. Hence, frequent collisions, obstinate envenomed, and bloody contests. The nation, prompted by ill-will and resentment, sometimes impels to war the government, contrary to the best calculations of policy. The government sometimes participates in the national propensity, and adopts through passion what reason would reject; at other times, it makes the animosity of the nation subservient to projects of hostility instigated by pride, ambition, and other sinister and pernicious motives. The peace often, sometimes perhaps the liberty, of nations has been the victim.

So likewise, a passionate attachment of one nation for another produces a variety of evils. Sympathy for the favorite nation, facilitating the illusion of a imaginary common interest in cases where no real common interest exists, and infusion into one other enmities of the other, betrays the former into a participation in the quarrels and wars of the latter, without adequate inducement or justification. It leads also to concessions to the favorite nation of privileges denied to others, which is apt double to injure the nation making the concessions, by unnecessarily parting with what ought to have been retained, and by exciting jealously, ill-will and a disposition to retaliate in the parties from who equal privileges are withheld. And it gives to ambitious, corrupted, or deluded citizens (who devote themselves to the favorite nation,) facility to betray or sacrifice the interests of their own **country**, without odium, sometimes even with popularity, gilding with the appearances of a virtuous sense of obligation, a commendable deference for public opinion, or a laudable zeal for public good, the base or foolish compliances of ambition, corruption, or infatuation.

As avenues to foreign influence in innumerable ways, such attachments are particularly alarming to the truly enlightened and independent patriot. How many opportunities do they afford to tamper with domestic factions, to practise the arts of seduction, to mislead public opinion, to influence or awe the public councils! Such an attachment of a small or weak towards a great and powerful nation dooms the former to be the satellite of the latter.

Against the insidious wiles of foreign influence (I conjure you to believe me, fellow-citizens), the jealously of a free people ought to be constantly awake, since history and experience prove that foreign influence is one of the most baneful foes of republican government. But that jealousy, to be useful, must be impartial; else it becomes the instrument of the very influence to be avoided, instead of a defence against it. Excessive partiality for one foreign nation, and excessive dislike of another, cause those whom they actuate to see danger only on one side, and serve to veil and even second the arts of influence on the other. Real patriots, who may resist the intrigues of the favorite, are liable to become suspected and odious; while its tools and dupes usurp the applause and confidence of the people to surrender their interests.

The great rule of conduct for us, in regard to foreign nations, is, in extending our commercial relations, to have with them as little political connection as possible. So far as we have already formed engagements, let them be fulfilled with perfect good faith. Here let us stop.

—George Washington

11

Democrats and Republicans

Dear Chris,

In the United States, the party of the left is the **democrats**, and that of the right the **republicans**. Both tend to hover close to the center, which is where they perceive the bulk of the voters to be.

A popular shorthand view of the two parties is that the democrats are the party of the poor and the republicans the party of the rich. Many democrats and republicans rebel against this shorthand view, and justifiably so, it's an over-simplification, but it is nevertheless a popular view. Generally, the left is more vocal in its concerns about the poor than is the right. Also, their approaches are different. In general, the left focuses on making the poor as comfortable as possible; the right focuses on trying to do something to reduce poverty.

The promises made by politicians during election campaigns have little to do with their conduct in office. Conservative Richard Nixon enacted leftist wage-price controls; liberal Lyndon Johnson sent thousands of troops to Vietnam.

The two political parties are really just marketing agencies. They select, package, and promote whatever candidates they believe can win; they use the sales pitches they believe will work.

Both parties are seekers of political power. They wish to control you, they disagree only over the specific types of control. In recent years the voters have come to understand this, hence the spate of bumper stickers referring to the demublicans and republicrats and to tweedle dum and tweedle dee.

In truth, the United States is a one-party country. The party has two branches, the republicans and democrats, and both branches have the same goal, to increase their scope and power; this has the net effect of increasing the scope and power of the government. In every election the one thing you can be certain about is that no matter which of the two main parties you vote for, the government will grow more powerful. When he took office in 1981, Ronald Reagan was the most strongly anti-government president of the 20th century. By the time he left in 1989, federal spending had doubled and the federal debt had nearly tripled.

Here is how republicans, democrats, socialists, welfare statists, communists, fascists, and capitalists fit on the commonly used political spectrum.

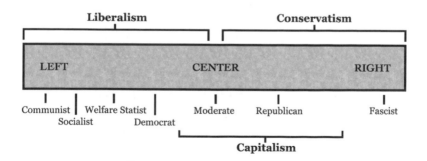

Capitalism is another word for free markets. It is an economic philosophy which says factories, land, office buildings, and the other sources of production and jobs should be owned by private individuals and companies, not government agencies. Capitalism says trade should be unrestricted, the forces of competition will prevent abuses much more effectively than government officials can if the officials permit competition to exist.

There are two kinds of **capitalists**, those who believe in capitalism and those who participate in it but don't believe in it. I suspect the latter are more numerous because nothing controls capitalists as effectively as capitalism does. The forces of competition are the most effective regulator and, as the great free-market economist Adam Smith pointed out, business people are always trying to find some way to reduce competition and boost profits. Many sing the praises of capitalism while they go hat in hand to government officials begging for special privileges and handouts. It's strange but true that some capitalists have done more to destroy capitalism and create socialism than socialists have.

Chris, in recent years a new political label has appeared, green. When the collapse of the Union of Soviet Socialist Republics occurred, leftists found themselves without an ideology to justify having more government. Millions moved swiftly into the environmental movement, which advocates extensive government controls to protect insects, plants, fish, and other organisms, and in some cases controls to protect even rocks and dirt. This is not to say everyone who wants to protect anything natural is a leftist, but in politics, the word green has a definite leftist slant. It implies a willingness or even strong desire to control your use of your property in the name of protecting nature.

Which brings me to the subjects of my next letter— socialism and communism.

Uncle Eric

12

Socialism and Communism

Dear Chris,

Socialism and communism may be the two most misleading labels in use today. In this letter I'll explain their popular
meanings, then their origin and true meanings.

In conversation today socialism is taken to be a kind of
advanced **liberalism**. A **socialist** is someone who wants vast
power over our economic affairs so that inequality of wealth
can be greatly reduced and poverty eliminated.

Communism is taken to mean the economic system of the
old Soviet Union, Red China, Cuba, and similar nations. An
extremely radical form of liberalism, communism is assumed
to be a ruthless police state little different than **Nazi** Germany.

These are the popular uses of the labels, but these uses are
far from the actual truth. To understand the real meanings we
need to know a bit about Karl Marx.

Marx (1818-1883) was a grossly incompetent economist
who tried to explain how the world works. In his COMMUNIST
MANIFESTO and other books, he developed his theory of the
development of human societies, **Marxism**. He even described a new kind of scientific analysis called "dialectical
materialism" which he claimed was superior to the cause-
and-effect analysis used by physicists, chemists, and other
scientists since time immemorial.

I won't get too deeply into dialectical materialism. It is nonsense and we should all be thankful automotive and aeronautical engineers don't use it; if they did we'd all be dead. In the former Soviet Union, scientists and engineers were once required to force their scientific work into the dialectical mold, which is why Soviet science and technology produced little of value and became the laughing stock of the world. Most of their "breakthroughs" were copies of work done in capitalist countries.

According to Marx's dialectical materialism, human society evolves through several stages. **Marxists** disagree about these stages, and about whether it is possible to skip one or two, or move back and forth, but here is the sequence I think most Marxists would accept. The first five stages do often happen as they are listed here:

1. Primitive slave state. No free trade or any other kind of freedom. The government owns and controls everything and everybody for the good of the government. People are property with no rights whatsoever. Life is short and filled with disease, cold, hunger, and filth.

2. Feudalism. Small independent kingdoms, some as small as one or two square miles, insulated from neighbors. Little free trade. The king or feudal lord owns all the land and has alliances with other kings and lords in the area. He controls the impoverished workers—the serfs—in whatever ways he wants, and takes heavy taxes from them. Much of the taxes go to finance the many wars in which he participates. A feudal kingdom is a self-sufficient island so completely cut off from the rest of the world that often a

serf will live his entire life without going more than five miles from home. Life is short and filled with disease, cold, hunger, and filth.

3. Mercantilism. Large nations with large governments much like those of today. Rulers believe money is wealth, and they arrange taxes and trade restrictions to cause goods to be exported so that money can be imported and collected to fill the government's coffers. Enormous wars. Some free trade is allowed, and the government does have some limited respect for the individual's rights to his life, liberty, and property, but taxes are heavy. Life is short and filled with disease, cold, hunger, and filth. The early American colonies were founded on mercantilism.

4. Capitalism. Great emphasis on free trade and limited government. Widespread respect and, in some cases, reverence for the individual's rights to his life, liberty, and property. Capitalism is the stage in which massive amounts of savings are accumulated because taxes are low. The savings are available for what economists call "capital formation"—the creation of large machines, farms, factories, offices, and other sources of jobs and production. Under capitalism life spans lengthen as the tools finally become available to conquer disease, cold, hunger, and filth. Marxists believe capitalism is hard on workers because employers earn more money than workers do. It may not be an exaggeration to say the American Revolution was a war to legalize capitalism.

5. Socialism. No free trade or any other kind of freedom. Socialism, says Marxist theory, is a transitional stage between capitalism and communism. It is a "dictatorship of the proletariat" (dictatorship of the working class) in which everything and everybody is owned and controlled by the government for the "good of society." The purpose of socialism, says Marxist theory, is to prepare the way for communism; this justifies whatever brutal means are necessary to make socialism work. The nations of the old Soviet Empire were the test beds for various degrees of socialism. They all fell apart.

6. Communism. This, says Marxist theory, is the utopian end-stage of socialism in which government has vanished and we all live happily ever after under the rule, "from each according to his ability, to each according to his need." You work as hard as you can to produce as much as you can, and contribute it all to the "common stock." You take from the common stock only what you need. The only places where true communism has ever appeared were a few religious monasteries, hippie communes, and other gatherings of idealists. Such cases have rarely lasted long because those who work hard find themselves supporting the lazy, and they leave. Realistically, a person can be a communist only in the sense that he is *striving* for the Marxist utopia. But the point to emphasize is that communism is an *ideal* in which there is *no government*. It's a form of anarchy, in the original sense of the word—no government. If the old Soviet

Union had been genuinely communist, with no government, it would have been the least threatening nation on earth.

Incidentally, politicians in the former USSR were no different than politicians anywhere else. They were seekers of political power. Once they got their hands on this power, they wanted to use it on someone. Marxist theory was their excuse.

But that's all "communism" was, an excuse, a scam. I've seen no evidence that these gangsters ever were really dedicated to any ideology or plan, except the plan to acquire and use power. The Soviet government was a typical garden variety tyranny little different than those of Hitler, Gengis Kahn, or Julius Caesar. It was just wrapped in Marxist packaging.

Some Americans thought there was substance to the "communist" facade, and many are still fearful of it. But it was mostly just hot air. The socialist agenda was followed to a large extent only because it required the use of massive amounts of power—the taxes, regulations, and wars that powerseekers have loved for thousands of years.

As you can imagine, leftists are embarrassed when someone points out that their economic philosophy helped lead to the murder of millions of innocent people in the Soviet Union. This may be why some writers began to write as if socialism and communism were two entirely different systems. They discarded the theory of society evolving from capitalism to socialism to communism. The system in the former USSR was called communism and was seen as cruel and warlike, while socialism was (still is) regarded by many as gentle, enlightened, and caring, a way to fight poverty.

This redefinition of the terms confused the debate. Many conservatives wound up spending their time and energy railing against communism, which didn't exist. And the assumption that the system in the former USSR was communist led to the impression among many that socialism *is* mild and gentle without the tendency to degenerate into brutality like communism. Socialism appeared more reasonable, and when socialist programs were proposed, conservatives would tolerate them saying, "well at least they aren't communist." That's how we got, for instance, Social Security and our mountainous Social Security taxes.

More Correct Location for Socialism and Communism

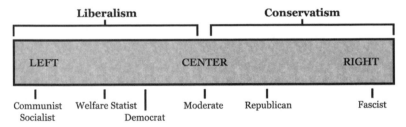

Welfare statism is a form of socialism and it is the most common kind of leftism in the United States. Almost everyone has some kind of pet socialist program. If it isn't Social Security it's Medicare, Aid To Families With Dependent Children, or something else.

Until the 1930s, few Americans believed in any of this. They supported private charities. In fact, Americans have long been known as the most charitable people on earth. But during the Great Depression they were so deeply shaken by an unemployment rate of 25% that most are now afraid to be without some kind of government "safety net." The aggregate of all these pet socialist safety nets has given a leftward bias to the U.S. economy. Conservatives did little to stop it, they were busy tilting at communist windmills.[12]

The most pathetic part of this confusion over socialism and communism concerns the U.S. military. Thousands of naive young soldiers were sent to fight "communism" in Korea, Vietnam, and other foreign nations when no such enemy existed. While the real enemy, socialism, was gradually taking over their homeland without a shot being fired. They understood none of it, they knew only that they had been thrown into the middle of something that was completely insane.

I was one of them, Chris. I remember the day it dawned on me. I was, I believe, 22 years old. During the Vietnam War I had joined the Air Force to fight communism. After two years, I suddenly realized that the "communists" we were fighting weren't literate enough to understand Marxist theory. They were just a bunch of soldiers like us, fighting and dying because their leaders said it was necessary.

In my next letter, fascism.

Uncle Eric

---

[12] Tilting at windmills is an expression from Cervantes' 1605 novel about Don Quixote. Tilting refers to medieval jousting by knights on horses. Don Quixote went about the countryside tilting at windmills, which he took to be dragons.

13

Fascism

Dear Chris,

Fascism is unique among the "isms" in that it has no intellectual leadership. Conservatives have Adam Smith, socialists have Karl Marx, and welfare statists have John Maynard Keynes; fascists have no one. Fascism is anti-intellectual. Its basic premise is that all truth is a matter of opinion and there's no sense discussing it; what counts is action.

The **fascist** worships power. Because all truth is mere opinion, right and wrong are, too. There is no real good or evil and no justice. The only thing that counts is who wins. Might makes right. History books are written by the victors.

Being anti-intellectual, the only leaders the fascists have are the activists who have tried to apply this no-truth philosophy. Tops among them was Adolph Hitler followed by Mussolini, Franco, and Tojo of World War II fame.

Fascism is a second type of socialism—socialism of the right. The German Nazis were fascist, and Nazi means National Socialist German Workers Party.

Like socialism of the left, socialism of the right means government controls everything and everybody. But unlike leftist socialism, fascism has no scientific theory and no view of the development of human society. It's just a pseudopatriotic, paranoid philosophy of hate. Kill or be killed. War is beautiful and conquest is utopia.

Fascists regard the government and the country as the same thing—The State—and they are totally dedicated to it. They tend to be intolerant of minorities, and they want a strong, charismatic leader.

Because he believes that truth, justice, right, and wrong are just matters of opinion, the fascist has a totally pragmatic view. He believes powerholders should do anything that appears necessary. Anything, no exceptions. He recognizes no moral limits because morality is just opinion.

If raising taxes appears necessary, the fascist wants to raise taxes. If lowering them appears necessary, he will lower them. If raising the taxes of some and lowering those of others appears necessary, he'll do it. He cares nothing about right or wrong, good or evil, only what appears necessary.

Necessary for what? For the state. For society. For the national interest. For the social good.

For whatever the powerholders decide.

Maybe even just for the fun of it.

When Mussolini was asked the fascist plan for Italy, he replied, "Our program is simple: we wish to govern Italy. They ask us for programs, but there are already too many. It is not programs that are wanting for the salvation of Italy, but men and will power."

Mussolini was Il Duce, "the leader," and he proudly boasted, "We have buried the putrid corpse of liberty!" In Italy *he* made all the decisions and *he* decided what was necessary. Famous slogans of Italy's fascism were, "credere, obbedire, combattere" ("to have faith, to obey, to fight") and "Mussolini ha sempre ragione ("Mussolini is always right").

Under fascism, if lying appears necessary, the powerholder will lie; if truthfulness appears necessary, he will be truthful. If freedom appears necessary, he grants freedom, and if slavery appears necessary, slavery it is.

If freedom for some and slavery for others appears necessary, that's okay, and if sending millions to death camps appears necessary, why not? Who's to say it's wrong? Truth and justice are matters of opinion.

Perhaps the most dangerous characteristic of fascism is that it can appear as any other philosophy. Fascists are masters of disguise. At any given moment they can decide use of another philosophy is temporarily necessary.

If capitalism appears necessary, the nation will have capitalism; if a welfare state appears necessary, a welfare state it will be.

The "reforms" undertaken in China and the Soviet Union during the 1980s were textbook examples of fascism in action. When Chinese rulers believed a measure of freedom was necessary, they granted freedom, and when they decided shooting people was necessary, the killing began.

In short, people can think they have liberty when they are actually living under fascism. Their "liberty" will vanish the moment powerholders decide it's necessary. The mailed fist in the velvet glove.

In World War II, 120,000 Japanese-Americans were sent to prison camps for no reason other than that they were Japanese-American (70% were American citizens).[13] None had been discovered doing anything harmful. This was a clear violation of the Bill of Rights, yet the President ordered it,

---

[13] See MANZANAR by John Hershey with photographs by Ansel Adams, published by Random House. Out of print. See also Roy Uyeda's story available from Bluestocking Press.

Congress approved it and the Supreme Court upheld it. Officials in all three branches got away with it cleanly because it was held to be necessary. Interesting precedent? Think about it.

Remember Oliver North and the Iran-Contra affair during the mid-1980s. Since 1979, the U.S. had been in an undeclared war with Iran; thousands of sailors and Marines were on warships in the Persian Gulf and hundreds of Marines had been killed by Iranian-backed terrorists. Nevertheless, marine Colonel North had been helping top officials supply missiles to the Iranians—the enemy—but no one was tried for treason. Officials said they were doing what they thought was necessary to gain release of a few hostages and money for the Contras in Nicaragua. This was considered sufficient explanation to excuse them.

They thought supplying weapons to the enemy was necessary, and this made it okay. Think about it.

Perhaps the best-kept secret of the twentieth century is that although Hitler's army was defeated and he died, the *basic principle he was fighting for has swept the world.*

Listen closely to political debate. In virtually every case you will hear the various sides all agreeing on the premise that powerholders should do whatever appears necessary. They disagree only on the details. This is their core question, what is necessary? Not, what is right and wrong?

No one tries to discover boundaries that must not be violated, they've given up belief in boundaries. All truth is relative. Good and bad are just opinion.

There is no line they will not cross if they think it appears necessary, as long as they can persuade the majority to vote for it. That's the determinant of right and wrong—whatever the majority says.

But Thomas Jefferson pointed out: "It is strangely absurd to suppose that a million human beings collected together are not under the same moral laws which bind each of them separately."

Of course, despite the victory of fascism, no one who practices it uses the word to describe his or her philosophy. Hitler gave fascism a bad name.

I'll finish this letter with this thought. Fascism is the most corrupting of all political systems. This is why the crimes of Nazi Germany were so shocking. If a primitive society had created these death camps the world would not have been so surprised, but Germany was one of the most advanced nations on earth, a leader in science, technology, and the arts. Germans were educated, but they fell into the habit of doing whatever appeared necessary.

Uncle Eric

"A departure from principle in one instance becomes a precedent for a second; that second for a third; and so on, till the bulk of society is reduced to mere automatons of misery, to have no sensibilities left but for sinning and suffering."
—Thomas Jefferson, 1816

14

What Are They Really?

Dear Chris,

In the early 1990s, we suddenly began to see renewed interest in capitalism in dozens of countries. What happened?

That's when the Soviet Empire was disintegrating. You may remember that during the 1989 breakup, Romania, one of the most ruthless of the Soviet-bloc dictatorships, went through a bloody uprising. President Ceausescu was captured and killed.

Suddenly leftists around the globe were moving to the right. We began hearing a chorus of praise for free markets.

More importantly, the words were backed by deeds. Taxes and trade restrictions were lowered. Protections for private property were strengthened.

American investors were approached by legions of financial advisors telling them to pour their hard-earned money into the new capitalist economies springing up like mushrooms on every continent.

Should you invest your money in some of these newly capitalist nations? Let's apply a little test first.

Uncle Eric's
Capital Risk Test

1. Does the nation have a constitution or some other legal safeguard based at least approximately on the fundamental principles of the old British common law?

2. Does this constitution provide explicit protection for the individual's rights to his life, liberty, and property?

3. Does this constitution protect the right to keep and bear arms?

4. Are the people so dedicated to this constitution that they will fight and die for it?

5. Are the protections for the individual's rights difficult to abolish? Does the constitution assume these rights are granted by a Higher Authority than the government?

6. Is free trade protected?

7. Does this constitution protect the individual's right to say anything he pleases about the government?

If the answer to any of these questions is "No," be very cautious. The rulers of the nation may be turning to free markets not because they believe liberty is morally right but because they do not want to end up like Ceausescu. They are fascists doing what they think is necessary at the moment.

Let me emphasize, at the moment. Any day with no warning they could change their minds, declare a state of emergency, and return to the former tyranny. This could include confiscating everything they can get their hands on including the investments of Americans.

This is not to say you should not invest in these nations. If you are a gambler who likes high-risk speculations, these nations are for you. As naive Americans pour in money, these nations become economic hot spots where big profits can be earned. But don't get into anything you can't get out of fast, and don't risk money you can't afford to lose. A nation that flunks our little seven-question test is not a genuine investment opportunity, it's a casino.

Incidentally, do you find this test unsettling? America no longer scores very well on it either. The Founders did their best to cement the fundamental principles of liberty into their Constitution and Bill of Rights, and they did a good enough job for it to last a long time. But those principles are almost gone now and the momentum the Founders gave us is fading. I hope you'll do all you can to spread the word about the urgent need to reverse course.

Uncle Eric

P.S. By the way, Chris, think about this. Many of these same Americans who freely choose to risk their capital in these nations would undoubtedly scream for the United States Government to do something to save their investment. This is an example of how wars, many wars, are born.

Here's a good research project. How many Marines have died protecting American liberty? How many have died protecting someone's foreign investments? A good place to start is with the list of 137 United States military actions since 1798 on page 24 of the January 15, 1987 WALL STREET JOURNAL. Ask a librarian to help you locate the article. Or visit these online sources: http://history.navy.mil/wars/foabroad.htm and http://history.navy.mil/faqs/faq56-1.htm

15

The Other Middle View

Dear Chris,

I will spend more time on juris naturalism in this letter and a few others because, as I said earlier, this side of the story has been almost forgotten, and if you don't get it from me you'll probably never get it.

Like moderates, juris naturalists combine left and right.

Moderates combine the left's desire to encroach on your economic affairs and the right's desire to encroach on your social affairs. Most Americans cluster around this moderate position. No one knows why, the assumption is that this is the location they find least offensive. In elections most people don't vote and those who do vote seem to be voting against, not for.

Juris naturalists are the opposite of moderates, they combine the left's desire for liberty in social affairs and the right's desire for liberty in economic affairs.

Chris, you asked earlier why the juris naturalist view wasn't represented on the left-right spectrum. This is because the spectrum contains no place for it. From far left to far right it's all statist. To show the location of the juris naturalist view, the spectrum needs to be altered.

A good way to place juris naturalism on the political spectrum is to split the spectrum in the middle, like so...

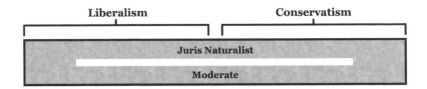

... then pull it apart, like so.

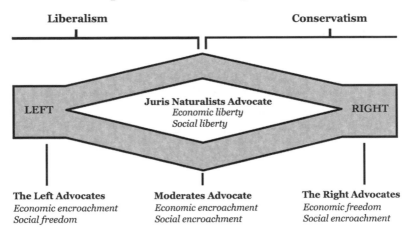

This split spectrum shows that juris naturalists and moderates are vastly different despite their central locations.

Notice I've shown that left and right speak of freedom while juris naturalists speak of liberty. America's Founders believed in absolutes, there are lines that must never be crossed.

In actual practice they had trouble adhering to this standard. Power corrupted them just as it corrupted anyone else. But they did believe in it. They believed in "natural rights," rights endowed not by government but by the Creator.

> The natural rights of the colonists are these: First, a right to life; second, to liberty; third to property; together with the right to support and defend them in the best manner they can.
> —Sam Adams

The Founders believed in a Higher Law than any government's law.

> Good and wise men, in all ages, ... have supposed that the Deity ... has constituted an eternal and immutable law, which is indispensably obligatory upon all mankind, prior to any human institution whatever.
> —Alexander Hamilton

They believed this law often renders human law invalid.

> Rightful liberty is unobstructed action according to our will within limits drawn around us by the equal rights of others. I do not add "within the limits of the law," for law is often but the tyrant's will, and always so when it violates the rights of an individual.
>
> —Thomas Jefferson

Juris naturalists are terrified of political power, they consider it the most evil drug ever discovered.

America's Founders believed no one could be trusted with political power. No one — no individual, no group, and no majority. They realized a person who would never dream of stealing from you himself will nevertheless vote to have a government agency do it for him. The Founders tried to create a government so small and weak that no one who got control would be able to do much damage. That's juris naturalism.

Until the 20th century the effort to have a small, harmless government was generally successful. The Federal government was so tiny it needed no income tax. Hard to believe, but true. It was financed entirely through liquor, tobacco, and import taxes. America became legendary as the most free and prosperous land ever known. Here political power was limited, and millions of immigrants risked their lives traveling thousands of miles to reach our shores.

This is not to say I agree with everything all juris naturalists say, I don't. But of all the viewpoints, that of the juris naturalist seems to me to be the most realistic. It's the one that sees humans the way they really are, fallible and corruptible, and it's the only viewpoint that has a moral compass.

You can test this yourself. Ask any non-juris naturalist what the basic moral principles of his political philosophy are. Where does he draw the lines the government should never cross?

As you know from my previous set of letters on law and government, the juris naturalist has an answer to this question. But I don't know any other philosophy that does. Or, I should say, others do, but they also have a set of exceptions that is so large it renders their principles meaningless.

Uncle Eric

16

The National Religion

Dear Chris,

Political power is the privilege of playing God. Today liberals, moderates, and conservatives are obsessed with obtaining this privilege, it's become the national religion. Ask any question, cite any social problem and the answer will be "there oughta be a law!"

In early America the churches were the centers of the communities and the clergy were the community leaders. When problems arose, people met at their local houses of worship to organize solutions. Now when problems arise, people write their congressional representatives. They demand that officials do whatever appears necessary. Congress receives about 87 million pieces of mail annually.[14]

This near total victory of the fascist principle is the reason juris naturalism has almost vanished. Like America's Founders, today's juris naturalist sees political power as evil. This does not make him popular in a land where political power has become the answer to everything.

---

[14] Source: http://www.thecapitol.net/FAQ/uc2_7.htm

Chris, you might be hearing a lot about **empowerment**. This is the latest panacea. If someone is hungry, cold, sick, or otherwise downtrodden, this is because he has not been sufficiently empowered. We must get him involved in politics, show him the advantages of encroaching on others.

Juris naturalists want all the same things everyone else wants. They deplore unemployment and poverty. They want children to be well educated. They hate drug addiction and war.

Their viewpoint differs from the others only in that juris naturalists believe problems should be solved through voluntary means, not politics.

As I think you've gathered from my previous set of letters I believe that our problems with business failures, unemployment, poverty, and all the rest are, at bottom, problems of character. More government controls will not solve them. If the people are gentle and honorable, controls will not be necessary; if they are not gentle and honorable, controls will be useless. In fact, if they are not gentle and honorable, controls will be dangerous; the cruel and corrupt will grab the reigns of power and create more tyranny and poverty.

Chris, the only real solution to our country's problems is to debunk the national religion, statism, and get back to the fundamental principles that yield strong character.

To help you identify the liberal and conservative slants in written material, my next letter will give you examples of how three writers, one leftist, one rightist, and one juris naturalist might have viewed one of the most important questions of the twentieth century. It arose during World War II.

Uncle Eric

17

A U.S.-Nazi Alliance
or
A U.S-Soviet Alliance?

Dear Chris,

As promised, here's an example of how writers of the liberal, conservative, and juris naturalist viewpoints might write about the big question America faced in World War II. First I'll give you some background.

Background

World War II began in 1931 with the Japanese attack on Manchuria. This was followed by war in Ethiopia (1935), Spain (1936), Finland (1939), and other areas until most of the world was involved.

The total number of people killed in the war was 40-50 million. Half were Soviet and German, mostly Soviet. U.S. losses were about 298,000, equal to less than two percent of the Soviet losses.

In short, World War II was primarily a battle between left and right, between fascist Hitler (the Axis powers) and socialist Stalin (the Allies).

This is not to say the participation of England, America, Japan, and other nations was unimportant. It is only to say that compared to the bloodbath that was happening between Hitler and Stalin all the rest was minor. Even the Battle of Midway and the Invasion of Normandy, although horrific, were tame compared to what was happening on the Eastern Front. In a single battle, at Stalingrad, 1.11 million people were killed. That's almost equal to America's losses in all the wars it has ever fought. Eleven thousand aircraft were involved at Stalingrad. Try to imagine it—one battle that went on for five *months*.

In the 1930s, as Hitler and Stalin began to square off, American political leaders began to ask, whose side should we take?

The three viewpoints follow:

The Leftist View

We must take sides with Stalin. Socialism is the wave of the future, it offers hope to the poor. Granted, socialism does require coercion, but once the system is in full operation we are confident it will create a highly advanced new civilization that will far surpass that of the capitalist West. Besides, Hitler is a barbarian and a bigot who murders Jews and other innocent people. He wants to take over the world.

The Rightist View

We must back Hitler. His fascist reforms in Germany have already reduced unemployment and put the German economy back on its feet. Also, millions of Americans are of German and Italian descent, many are in sympathy with the Axis powers.

True, Hitler isn't perfect, but Stalin is certainly worse; we know the Soviet socialists have murdered millions more than the Nazis have. Besides, Stalin wants to take over the world, too.

The Juris Naturalist View

Why get into this war? The German Nazis and Soviet socialists are both murderous barbarians. If they wish to batter each other into dust, why should we interfere?

There's nothing new happening. Most of the nations of the world have been fighting insane wars for thousands of years. Thomas Jefferson called the Europeans "nations of eternal war" and advised us never to get involved with them. George Washington warned against foreign political involvement in his FAREWELL ADDRESS. We cannot clean up the world.

The only rational approach is to stay out, remain neutral the way the Swiss do. If we use our mighty industrial capacity to back one side, that side will win and it will then be strong enough to menace the world. Let them pulverize each other.

The Japanese have joined the Nazis, but we must allow free trade with everyone. Should we levy trade restrictions or an oil embargo on the Japanese, or freeze their assets, we might damage their economy and provoke them to attack us. We'd be dragged into the war.

The Outcome

The leftist view was the most popular in America due to the perceived success of Franklin Roosevelt's New Deal.[15] So, the leftist view prevailed in the war.

Thousands of Americans recruited by the Communist Party in 1936 fought against the fascists in Spain. After Hitler and Stalin finally went head to head in June, 1941, U.S. officials backed Stalin.

United States officials enacted trade restrictions, an oil embargo, and a freeze against the Japanese. In July 1941, China's Flying Tiger air force squadrons fighting the Japanese were financed and supplied by the United States Government in violation of the United States Neutrality Act. The Flying Tigers were equipped with American planes flown by American pilots. On December 7, 1941, the Japanese retaliated by attacking Pearl Harbor; America was in the war.

With the help of massive shipments of United States weapons and supplies, Stalin emerged triumphant. Then, for 45 years after 1945, the world lived in fear of the Soviet Empire. This empire was little different than Hitler's, except that it was worse; the Soviet socialists murdered more people than Hitler's Nazis did. (The commonly cited death tolls are, Hitler 20.9 million, Stalin 42.6 million.)

---

[15] Widely taught in our government-controlled school system is the assertion that the New Deal stopped the Great Depression. The fact is that the depression was stopped by World War II. The New Deal not only failed, it prevented the depression from ending until the New Deal itself was ended. The government's own statistics now show that more Americans were unemployed in 1940 than in 1931.

Chris, many tend to assume political ideas are mere ivory tower theories for scholars to debate, but this is quite wrong and dangerous. As World War II demonstrated, these ideas are life and death matters that affect us and our families directly. A single bad idea can corrupt and kill millions.

Before we leave the subject of war, let me point out how important it is to be aware of the unusual psychology of Americans.

Until 9-11[16], the United States had not been faced with a serious threat of invasion since the War of 1812. No living American had experienced war in his homeland, and Americans had come to believe peace and prosperity were the normal state of affairs for humans. When a war broke out somewhere, many Americans believed we should get into it on the side of the good guys and bring it to a swift conclusion.

The fact is that the normal state of affairs almost everywhere except America is war and poverty. I once read that in the past 3,000 years, the earth has been without a major war for eight percent of the time. That eight percent sounds high to me, I'd doubt it's as much as one percent.

Equally important is the fact that few wars are contests between good guys and bad guys. Most are between bad guys and bad guys, as World War II was. Taking sides with the lesser of the two evils is simply a way to strengthen the lesser evil so that it becomes the greater. Chris, what can be gained by that?

---

[16] On September 11, 2001, in an attack against the United States, over 3000 civilians were murdered. The World Trade Center in New York was destroyed, as well as a portion of the Pentagon. Four civilian airliners were destroyed, including passengers and crew. This attack is also referred to as Sept. 11, Sept. 11 Attack, and 9-11.

As I said in an earlier letter, when I give you this side of the story I'm not arguing for isolationism. I'd like to see Americans travel everywhere and do business and make friends in every country. But, like America's Founders, I'm against political connections, they only get us into trouble. In short, if a foreign government calls, don't answer the phone. As you read earlier, George Washington had a great deal more to say about this in his FAREWELL ADDRESS.[17]

Incidentally, in an attempt to discredit America's Founders, statists frequently argue that the Founders' viewpoints, over two centuries old, are supposedly outdated and no longer apply to a modern world. Juris naturalists know the Founders studied civilizations and their governments, both ancient and contemporary, as well as human nature. The Founders designed a system of government to protect individual liberty from the weaknesses of basic human nature, which they found unchanging in light of history.

Uncle Eric

---

[17] WASHINGTON'S FAREWELL ADDRESS, see pages 55-57.

18

Economic Counterparts

Dear Chris,

Most of politics is concerned with taxing and redistributing wealth. America's Founders believed government was a necessary evil. They knew that taxation went hand-in-hand with government. They tried to keep both small.

Until the 20th century when income tax was created, the Federal government's tax receipts were nearly 100% from taxes on liquor, tobacco and imports. Today these taxes account for only 3% of the Federal government's receipts, which means that 97% of the Federal government's income today is from taxes loaded on top of what America's Founder's originally created.

The various political philosophies are heavily dedicated to deciding who the money should be taken from and to whom it should be given. Hence economics is basic to the political philosophies.

The economics of the far left is socialism, or Marxism.

Moving from extreme left to center-left, the economics of the democrats, welfare statists, and most moderates is called **Keynesianism** (Kaynz-ee-an-izm). Invented by economist John Maynard Keynes during the 1930s, Keynesianism is a kind of compromise socialism.

Keynes was a brilliantly persuasive salesperson but not much of an economist. He was reasonably sure the cause of the Great Depression was government controls on the economy, so to cure the depression he prescribed more government controls. It didn't make sense but it was exactly what powerseekers wanted to hear—they bought it lock, stock, and barrel.

To be fair I should point out that Keynes never gave carte blanche for all government controls. By today's standards he was conservative. But he opened the flood gates and today the welfare state policies that produce so much economic disruption and poverty carry his name.

Moving to the right, the economics of the conservatives is called **monetarism**. Its focus is on the quantity of money in the economy. **Monetarists** blame the Great Depression and other economic problems on the government's manipulation of the money supply.

Monetarists tend to believe in capitalism. They want to see taxes lowered and economic controls lifted. In recent years they've also been sniffing at the fringes of juris naturalism. They are beginning to suspect that the root cause of high business failure rates and high poverty rates is political power.

The far right, the fascists, have no economic theory except, do whatever appears necessary.

The economics of the juris naturalists is called **Austrian economics** because the founders of this economic viewpoint were from Austria.

Austrian economics is the modern version of **laissez faire** capitalism. The origin of the French term laissez faire is instructive. During the 1600s, Louis XIV wanted to see business conditions improved and poverty reduced. Many government controls were in force but the economy wasn't working well, so he told finance minister Jean Baptiste Colbert to do something about it. Colbert called a meeting of French businessmen to ask what the government could do to improve the economy. The businessmen conferred and came up with the answer, if you want to improve the economy *laissez nous faire* (leave us alone).

For the first 150 years of United States history, laissez faire was the dominant economic and legal viewpoint, which is why the country became legendary as the most free and prosperous land ever known. Not that laissez faire was ever totally in operation, there were some taxes, controls, and special privileges, but this "land of opportunity" came closer to applying laissez faire than any other before or since. By 1900 this small agrarian nation had become an industrial powerhouse, the "land of opportunity" envied around the world. Millions of immigrants were pouring in.

Then the Great Depression hit. Economists at that time did not have a good understanding of depressions. Many jumped to the conclusion that depressions are an inevitable consequence of laissez faire. This greatly pleased the socialists.

By the 1930s, English had become the predominant world language. Ludwig von Mises (Mee-zis) and other economists in Austria had discovered the solution to depressions, but their works had not yet been translated into English. Keynes was British and had friends in high places. His theories swept the capitalist world.

Another factor working against the spread of the Austrian viewpoint was the Austrian economists' penchant for asking embarrassing questions. Everyone says government is necessary, where is the evidence? asks the Austrians. Yes, we have plenty of evidence that law is necessary, but where is the evidence that the benefits of government are greater than the costs? A good economist should not jump to conclusions, say Austrian economists.

The embarrassing questions extend to specifics. Where is the evidence that government must issue the currency? That it must run the post office? The schools? The welfare system?

Every government program is a sacred cow to someone, which is why Austrian economists are rarely invited to Washington cocktail parties. No powerseeker wants to hear that the emperor has no clothes.

But times change. Socialism, Keynesianism, and monetarism have all been tried and found wanting, and now the only school left to try is the Austrian. Two Austrian school economists have been awarded Nobel prizes. America's Founders would be proud.

To juris naturalists, "taxation" is synonymous with stealing. Most people believe that as long as the majority or their elected representatives vote for it, taxation isn't stealing, and that makes it okay, so don't complain. You might think about these questions in trying to sort out your own beliefs:

Is there an upper limit to taxation?

If so, how much of a family's income do you think the government can take before the taking becomes theft?

In my next letter we'll get more specific about your money.

Uncle Eric

P.S. If you would like to learn more, the Foundation for Economic Education (Irvington-On-Hudson, NY 10533) publishes many books and articles about Austrian economics.

19

Effects on Your Money

Dear Chris,

The various political philosophies and their economic counterparts affect your pocketbook in different ways. In most cases, the leftist policies are the most destructive. Liberals seem to be more interested in good intentions than good results, so they are willing to enact higher taxes, more controls, or whatever else they believe is necessary to fight poverty.

If you own a business, leftist policies can mean big trouble. Liberals see business as a predatory activity and they view a business's income as a kind of inexhaustible ore deposit they can mine.

Liberals are equally dangerous if you are an employee. You won't benefit much if they tax or control your employer out of business, even if they do it with good intentions.

Also, liberals are pro-union, and pro-union often means anti-labor. A union is a middleman that wholesales your labor to the employer. It stands between you and the employer and prevents you from negotiating your wage or working conditions on an individual basis. Even if you are an outstanding worker, the union will see to it that your earnings are tied to the same wage scale as the workers who are mediocre or lazy.

Sometimes unions are granted legal privileges that enable them to force wages up to unrealistic levels. In these cases, employers find it economical to replace workers with machines, or sometimes to simply shut down their operations altogether, or send the operations overseas. Union officials grow more powerful, but the total number of workers with jobs is reduced.

I remember when I was growing up in the 1950s most of my uncles were union members and great believers in unions. This was during the heyday of unions. Even though a child at the time, I remember noticing that when a union went on strike, my uncles would say they were off work because "they" had decided to strike. It was never "us" making the decision, always "them," in an unwitting acknowledgment that my uncles had no control over their own destinies. Everything important was decided by the union, by "them." Even though my uncles believed in unions, I realized they nevertheless saw them as a form of mob rule.

Being advocates of Keynesian economics, liberals also have little fear of government borrowing, or of inflationary monetary policies. Government borrowing crowds private businesses out of the financial markets, destroying jobs; inflationary monetary policies reduce the value of the dollar, driving up prices.

The effect on investment markets can be devastating. Leftist monetary policies can cause wild swings in interest rates and in stock and bond values. All this is explained in my previous letters and other sources you can get from the Foundation for Economic Education.

Conservatives are less dangerous to your pocketbook in almost every way. Being more pragmatic, they have a better understanding of economics and they are less likely to interfere in your work, business, or investments.

However, conservatives have two major blind spots. First, their desire to use law to stamp out immorality leads them to want to keep a close eye on your behavior. The conservative war on drugs has brought huge reductions in privacy, especially financial privacy. To try to catch drug dealers, the government is moving toward trying to track virtually all transactions. This makes it easier for the IRS to collect more taxes.

This started during the Prohibition Era in the 1920s and '30s. Bootlegger Al Capone became so wealthy and powerful that police couldn't jail him for the Saint Valentine's Day massacre or other murders of which he was suspected. Desperate to do something about him, officials hit on the idea of auditing his tax returns; Capone was eventually captured and imprisoned for tax evasion.

From the Capone case, conservatives learned that a government can punish nearly any immoral person for any immorality if it can gather enough financial information. When powerseekers claim they want more financial information about us to fight drugs, pornography, prostitution, gambling, or other immoralities, conservatives cooperate. In effect, conservatives have joined liberals who want this information to enforce higher taxes and stricter economic regulations.

With the help of conservatives, government agencies have become voracious consumers of financial data. In his book MARK SKOUSEN'S COMPLETE GUIDE TO FINANCIAL PRIVACY, Skousen reports, "There are about 50 files kept on the average American," and the government can and does use all of them.

This emphasis on immorality is understandable, conservatives realize the line between immorality and crime is easy to cross, and they are afraid of crime. I don't blame them. I am, too, especially when I think of what could happen to my family. Fear can cause a person to want laws that control every movement of every individual.

This brings to mind a comment by Senator Joe Biden during one of Congress's periodic anti-crime fevers: "There is a mood here that if someone came to the floor and said we should barb-wire the ankles of anyone who jaywalks, I suspect it would pass."[18] In the wake of 9-11, the passage of the Patriot Act and other limitations of privacy have only made the situation worse.

Chris, you know my thinking. Crime is like almost all the other troubles in America today. It is, at bottom, a problem of character. If the character of the people does not improve, whatever else we do won't matter, and that includes enacting tough laws. In fact, asking government to solve problems by enacting more laws is asking for more of the cause of the problems. The more laws, the less justice.

Another blind spot of conservatives is war. Show them a **communist** and they are ready to send in the Marines. But war costs money, which means it leads to higher taxes.

So, conservatism is dangerous to your pocketbook but on balance, liberalism is far worse. What about juris naturalism?

Juris naturalists desire protection for your privacy in all matters both economic and social. They don't want you to be immoral but they believe laws enacted to fight most immorality will do more harm than good. As long as you keep your agreements and do not encroach on other people or their property, juris naturalists do not wish to use the force of law on you. They'll use peaceful persuasion, but no police, guns, or prisons. Juris naturalists hate taxes, controls, welfare,

---

[18] Quoted in NEWSWEEK, November 22, 1993, p.25.

subsidies, and every other government intrusion into your business, career, or investments.

Thousands of Americans are working to revive the philosophy of America's Founders, but the task is enormous and it is far from complete. For the time being, the world will continue to be dominated by liberals, moderates, and conservatives; theirs are the policies to which you must adapt. Grab your wallet with both hands and hang on tight.

By the way, most news stories and political and economic analysis we read today are based on the left-right political spectrum. Liberals versus conservatives. Who's winning, who's losing. This is helpful to some extent but you'll understand much more about how the world works if you focus not on liberals versus conservatives but on political power versus liberty.

Where is power winning and losing? Where is liberty winning and losing? This tells us much about the direction of the economy and our investments. Where liberty is winning, we find prosperity.

Uncle Eric

P.S. How can we replace government schools, police, courts, roads, and other "public" services with services that are voluntary? The problem has been researched for more than a half-century by the Foundation for Economic Education (web site: www.fee.org), the Cato Institute (web site: www.cato.org), and many other organizations. The how-to literature is vast. To learn the many ways of getting things done without the use of force, I suggest you start with the Reason Public Policy Institute (web site: www.privatization.org), or the Advocates (web site: www.theadvocates.org)

20

Three Types Of Wrongdoing

Dear Chris,

One way to look at the difference between juris natural-ists and others is to divide wrongdoing into three types.

First is bad **manners**. If you engage in bad manners, but no one notices, no harm is done.

Second is **immorality**, which concerns damage to your-self and perhaps to others. Immorality isn't good, says the juris naturalist, but it isn't always serious enough to warrant intervention by the heavy hand of the law.

Third is a **tort**, which is harm done to others that is serious enough to warrant intervention by the law. A tort is always immoral. A tort is the use of fraud, theft, or force. The act itself may not be especially severe, but it could lead to reprisals and escalation—a feud, as with the Hatfields and McCoys[19]—so the law can step in. This is not to say peaceful voluntary means should not be tried first, but if they fail, force of law can be used. Sparingly.

---

[19] The Hatfields and McCoys were two families in the Appalachian Mountains (West Virginia and Kentucky) who fought from about 1870 to 1900.

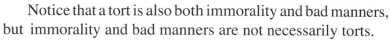

Notice that a tort is also both immorality and bad manners, but immorality and bad manners are not necessarily torts.

Okay, you say, but what about religious laws, shouldn't they be enforced by police and courts?

Those that deal with torts, yes. If someone kills or steals, these are torts, and I believe police and courts should do something about it.

But suppose someone shows disrespect for their parents, or does not observe a religious holiday. Would you want the police and courts involved? There was a day when they were. If you didn't go to church on Sunday you went to jail.

Would you be willing to pay your hard earned money for police and courts to throw people in jail for disrespecting their parents? Would you want them prying into your home life to be sure *you* aren't "misbehaving"?

We must draw a line somewhere. Law involves force, it is costly, clumsy, and usually damaging, and best used only in cases of serious harm done to others. Law is a last resort, so the juris naturalist draws the line at torts, at serious, measurable harm done to others. For combating immorality that does not harm others, less costly voluntary means are better.

Here I should mention the legal concepts of "clear and present danger," "consequential damage," and "probable cause."

As every biologist knows, virtually everything any person or animal does can affect every other person or animal indirectly. A butterfly happens by a campfire in the Amazon jungle just as a spark jumps from the fire. The puff of air from the insect's wings fans the spark into a flame. The flame grows into a forest fire. The forest fire throws so much ash and soot into the air that wind currents in the Gulf of Mexico are changed. The ultimate result of the butterfly's brief passage by the campfire is that Georgia is hit by a hurricane that destroys billions of dollars of property and kills dozens of people.

If the law were to be concerned with the possible indirect effects of our actions, we'd all be in court or in prison forever. So, courts use principles such as "clear and present danger," "consequential damage," and "probable cause" to decide if an act requires legal action.

Perhaps the most important idea separating juris naturalists from others is that in public policy matters the juris naturalist is concerned only about torts, while others will use legislation to try to control immoralities that are not torts, or even bad manners. I once read a news story about a prominent lawyer who seriously suggested that we should make a law against telling lawyer jokes. This was just after a lawyer had been murdered. The reasoning was that such jokes create disrespect for lawyers and this leads ultimately to lawyers being assaulted. The lawyer trying to pass the law was clearly not a juris naturalist.

In my next letter, I'll talk about other political labels and their meanings.

Uncle Eric

21

Muddied Waters

Dear Chris,

The collapse of the Soviet Empire has muddied the waters of political labels even more than did the Empire's rise. For instance, in Russia the word conservative means someone who wants to conserve the old order, socialism. A Russian conservative is, therefore, a leftist.

Russia isn't the only place where things are getting more confused. In England and parts of west Europe, the word liberal has been resurrected for its original meaning, juris naturalist.

So be careful. Don't assume you know how a word is being used. Always try to learn the writer's beliefs and definitions. I'm afraid that as conditions in Europe and Asia continue to change, the labels will too, they may not jell for decades.

Here are a few more political labels you may come across.

Anarchism. This is a good word to avoid. Originally it meant no government. Now it is sometimes used to mean chaos or terrorism. In Lebanon during the 1980s, at least 40 small governments were carving out their little empires and fighting with each other. Many press reports called this anarchy. How the presence of 40 governments can be called anarchy is a mystery to me, but the word has been twisted around to mean this to some people.

Terrorism. Avoid this word, too. The strict meaning of **terrorist** is a person who creates terror, usually through violence. But the word has been **politicized**. Now enemies regularly call each other terrorists. An old saying is that one man's terrorist is another man's freedom fighter. As far as I know, no major government has been innocent of deliberately killing innocent people. When you hear someone called a terrorist, always ask why he behaves this way. What's the history?

Warlord. This is another word that has been politicized. Originally a warlord was a high ranking military officer in charge of a medieval kingdom's military operations. Now the word "warlord" is like the word "terrorist." If you don't like the other side's politics or tactics, you call their leader a warlord.

Populist. I won't say you should avoid this word, it's not as fuzzy as anarchism or terrorism, but it's not very precise either. I cannot find a good definition of it anywhere. As it is used in the mainstream press, it seems to mean someone who is not a democrat or republican but claims to be popular with rank and file[20] voters.

---

[20] Rank and file: persons who are involved, but not in a leadership position.

Bolshevik. Originally a Bolshevik was a member of the Social Democratic Party of Russia around 1917, the time of the Russian Revolution. Later it came to mean any socialist or communist. Now that the Soviet Empire has fallen, the word is being used in various ways in Russia and no one is sure what it means. Best to avoid it.

Nationalist. An extremely patriotic person who regards his nation as being of supreme importance. Many nationalists will do whatever is good for their country even if this means harming innocent persons. Nationalism easily leads to war.

Civil Libertarian. Some leftists are so solidly in favor of freedom of speech, press, religion, and privacy that they have adopted a special label referring to these "civil liberties." They do some good work in helping to protect these liberties, but they generally have little interest in your right to free trade, your right to your property, or your right to keep the money you've earned.

Radical, Extremist, Fanatic. These words are commonly used to describe a person who is highly committed to a cause with which the speaker or writer does not agree. Is an American who wins the Medal of Honor a radical? An extremist? A fanatic? The enemy has often thought so. In 1776, the government's tax collectors regarded John Hancock as one of the most radical and extreme fanatics in America. The American rebels regarded Hancock, the "Prince of Smugglers," as a great patriot.

Chris, at this point I should also clear up some possible confusion over the word conservative. I recently got a letter from a friend who disagrees with my saying that conservatives are more militaristic than liberals. He points out that conservatives claim conservatism is the philosophy of peace. They look back at America's major wars of the 20th century — World War I, World War II, Korea, and Vietnam and note that in each case the president was a democrat, meaning a liberal or leftist.

Here's the 3-point reply that I wrote to him:

1. If you are referring to the "old right," that is, the pre-World War II conservatives who were trying to keep America out of war, I fully agree with you. I would like to see today's conservatives return to that philosophy of *neutrality*, which is now called *isolationism*.

2. Everything you say about liberal presidents getting us into wars is resoundingly true. But I believe a president is rarely representative of the philosophy he espouses. In fact, I believe most politicians see their political philosophies as sales tools, not real beliefs. Their philosophies are what they use to get elected. Once in office a president is quickly corrupted to the point that he becomes without any real philosophy at all. Ronald Reagan was probably the closest we've seen to the old right philosophy, but he jumped at the chance to get involved in military adventures in Grenada and Beirut, neither of which had anything to do with defending America. "Conservative" George H.W. Bush seemed to get a genuine high out of his

wars in Panama (1989-90) and Iraq (1990-91). If you look back at Vietnam, say 1965 to 1971, I think you'll find the voters divided rather cleanly along the lines of conservatives being *hawks* and liberals being *doves*. But, again, I'm speaking about the post-1941 right, not the old right.

3. During the 1930s, classical liberals lost ownership of the word liberal. Liberals were originally very much like the old right, but Franklin Roosevelt's New Deal turned the word liberal into something signifying socialism. Similarly, I think real conservatives have lost ownership of the word conservative, it no longer means what it did or what conservatives want it to mean.

To summarize, if by conservative you mean the old right, then I agree with you. But that is no longer the generally accepted meaning of the word.

When I use the words liberal and conservative, I use them as the mainstream press and general public uses them. That is, I (reluctantly) accept the fact that the meanings have been changed.

Chris, as I think you've gathered from this letter, communication is becoming more difficult every day. As the meanings of words are destroyed, talking and even thinking are becoming more difficult. To counter this, ask people to define their terms so that you know the real message they intend to convey. I can't emphasize this point enough. Ask people to define their terms.

Uncle Eric

22

Who Gets The Children?

Dear Chris,

Let me draw your attention to one of our country's biggest problems, bigotry.

No two humans are identical. We each have our own unique combinations of skin color, religion, sex, hair color, eye color, likes, dislikes, skills, character flaws, you name it.

There seems to be a tendency for persons who have roughly similar traits to group together and to reject others who have different traits. This "us against them" feeling is common around the world and throughout history.

Each of us is strange in someone's eyes.

But civilization has advanced to the point that all reasonable persons now know bigotry is harmful not only to the outsider who is being rejected but to the insiders, too. The outsider often has unusual, hard-to-find skills and talents that would benefit everyone if he were accepted into the group.

America has been the proof of this. A major reason this nation prospered for so long is that we accepted nearly anyone from anywhere, so we got a wide variety of enormously productive "strange" people. For the entire nineteenth century there was an enormous "brain drain" from the old world to the new.

But even the most open-minded, rational person some-times seems bigoted for a very good and understandable reason—children. Parents are protective of their young, and they become cautious or even frightened when their young are in the company of a stranger. What are this stranger's beliefs? His motives? His feelings? How will he behave?

Most people are quite tolerant, but not when their kids are involved. With their children—this is my key point—they want to always err on the side of caution. Even though they believe the odds are slim that a "strange" person would harm their child, they will take no chances.

They don't want "strange" people in the classroom teach-ing their kids. This is where the biggest concerns come from, the schools.

If all parents could choose the schools to which they send their children (and their money) then those who do not feel threatened by a particular kind of outsider could choose schools that are willing to hire these outsiders as teachers. Those who do feel threatened could choose schools where the outsiders are not hired.

But as long as parents cannot choose their own schools, those with strong feelings will try to make laws banning "strange" people from the whole society. They may not really want these people completely banned but, if that's the only way to keep the strangers out of the classroom, that's what many will try to do. Something that should be no more than a minor worry becomes a witch hunt.

Also, because the schools have been politicized, other things that never should be touched by politics are—religion, for instance. Should prayer be allowed in public (govern-ment-owned) schools? Some say yes, others no. It's become a political question because the teaching of the children is controlled by politics—not by the individual choice of the parents. The parents can choose their children's brand of shoes, their doctors and dentists, their milk, bread and vegetables, but not their schooling. The child's mind is a political football, fought over by everyone who wants to control children's minds.

Summarizing, many public issues are not what they seem. Often they are really about protecting children when parents are forced by law to expose the children to real or imagined threats. Give the children back to their parents and people will relax. A great deal of the bigotry will go away.

Chris, as I said in an earlier letter, I'm giving you a side of the story you've never heard before because if you don't get it from me you'll probably never get it anywhere. Rarely mentioned is the fact that many public issues simply go away once people are free to choose.[21]

If the law did not restrict choice, people could move in directions comfortable to them; they could spread out. But when their movement is restricted to certain channels, they end up colliding with the walls and with each other.

Liberty solves many problems.

Uncle Eric

---

[21] See FREE TO CHOOSE by Milton Friedman, a PBS series, as well as book by same title, published by Harvard University Press.

23

The Return of Racism

Dear Chris:

In my previous letter I wrote about bigotry. You might be interested in this short article that I wrote in 1994:

Recently I visited Orange County in Southern California. Didn't see any orange groves but did see two vacant lots. In Southern California these qualify as wilderness.

The occasion was my 30th high school reunion. It was great to see old friends but also sad. Things have changed, and not for the better. The old high school is a maze of fences and walls. I've seen prisons and military bases that were less heavily fortified. The night before the reunion someone torched the administration building. In our day this was every kid's fantasy, now they actually do it. No self-restraint. Rotten apples galore. Barbarism.

At the reunion, gazing across this crowd of some 400 middle-aged baby boomers, I was struck by how much progress America has lost.

This graduating class was of all colors. There, in Orange County in the mid-1960s, centuries of racism had been thrown into full retreat.

I'm white, and one of my good friends was black; the best man at my wedding was Mexican. Such interracial friendships were typical in this group.

At my wife's school nearby in 1964, the kids had elected a home coming queen who was white and a home coming king who was black. The parents went ballistic while the kids stood around wondering what all the shouting was about.

There, in those days, skin color was close to becoming just one more physical characteristic of no particular importance.

American law was becoming color blind.

The cause was our parents. Many in that generation were bigoted but they didn't feel good about it. Teachers, legal scholars, and, above all, the churches continually reminded them that bigotry was evil.

My parents' generation didn't change much but, for the most part, *they raised their kids differently.* Our graduating class was one of the first to show the results. We did not know it at the time, but we were the vanguard of a new era. The African-American, Asian-American, and Hispanic-American were on the way to being as accepted as the Irish-American and all others who had come before. I am entirely certain that if this natural progress had been allowed to continue, today in America there would be no racism except in a few isolated pockets.

But along came the government with its "affirmative action" in the 1970s and blew it all right out of the water. Suddenly my generation was *forced* to be aware of skin color.

The law was no longer color blind.

Today, race riots have demolished large parts of southern California and more are surely coming. Political power corrupts all it touches.

Every time the government attempts to handle our affairs, it costs more and the results are worse than if we had handled them ourselves.

—Benjamin Constant, 1818

Chris, as I said in my last letter, liberty solves many problems.

Uncle Eric

24

The First American Philosophies

Dear Chris:

The left-right or liberal-moderate-conservative political spectrum was not America's original political structure. In the late 1700s and early 1800s, it was the Federalists and—do you know who the other side was?

At one time or another almost every American hears of THE FEDERALIST PAPERS of Hamilton, Madison, and Jay, so they know of the Federalist political philosophy. They may not know what this philosophy was, but they know it existed.

Opposing the Federalists were the anti-Federalists.[22]

Patrick Henry and James Madison were on opposite sides of the constitutional debate in 1787, but both turned out to be right in their economic predictions.

Leader of the anti-Federalists, Patrick Henry was adamantly opposed to creation of the Federal government. He saw no need to burden Americans with another layer of government and, if this layer were added, he believed it would eventually "oppress and ruin them." He predicted a gigantic bureaucracy and military empire that would tax and

---

[22] See THE FEDERALIST PAPERS and THE ANTI-FEDERALIST PAPERS, published by New American Library, a division of Penguin Putnam, NY.

harass the people at home and lure them into wars abroad. Obviously, he turned out to be right.

Leader of the Federalists, James Madison was the architect of the Federal government. He said this new layer of government was needed in order to control the state governments. He feared the state democracies would evolve into mob rule—that is, into dictatorships of the majority—and they would eventually grow to tax and control every aspect of American life. He feared unemployment and widespread business failures if the power of the states continued to expand. He turned out to be right, too.

In other words, Henry and Madison were both mortally afraid of political power. Neither believed any human or group of humans could be trusted with it. They regarded it as a drug that would corrupt the morals and the judgment of all who acquired it. Both were trying to invent a system that would minimize it, and both knew the consequences if this drug ever came into wide use.

In their CATO LETTERS, which were popular among anti-Federalists and some Federalists, Thomas Gordon and John Trenchard wrote that political power "renders men wanton, insolent to others, and fond of themselves. ... All history affords but few instances of men trusted with power without abusing it."[23] James Burgh, another favorite of anti-Federalists and some Federalists, wrote, "Power is of an elastic nature, ever extending itself and encroaching on the liberties of the subjects."[24]

Are you shocked to learn that in 1787, Patrick Henry and many other great Americans were against creation of the

---

[23] The ANTI-FEDERALISTS by Jackson Turner Main, W.W. Norton & Co., New York, 1961, p.9
[24] Ibid.

Federal government? Do their concerns cause you to see the Federal government in a whole new light?

America's Founders were not gods or saints or angels. They were as human as you and me. They made mistakes. I believe their biggest was in failing to include protection for free trade in the First Amendment, which does include protection for freedom of speech, freedom of the press, and freedom of religion and assembly.

Henry and Madison both turned out to be right in their predictions about what political power would do to us if either the state or Federal governments ever grew very large, which they have.

Do I favor one side over the other? Not really.

Emotionally, I'm an anti-Federalist to the core. But rationally, I find it hard to disagree with the Federalists. For when we accept the fact that government will exist—that we have no choice in the matter because someone will set one up—then we are faced with the questions of who will set it up and what kind it will be. Anyone who is dedicated to the system of liberty can have only one answer. *We* want to set it up, and we want it to be the least dangerous type possible.

The job the Federalists did was not perfect but it was quite good. They invented a system that is so clumsy, disorganized, and inherently stupid that even the most intelligent powerseekers who have gotten control of it have had a terrible time forcing their schemes onto us.

Here's an important point. I strongly suspect that the conflict between the Federalists and anti-Federalists led to both sides together accidentally inventing a better system than either alone would have.

The Federalists were responsible for the main body of the Constitution, which is a masterpiece of political sabotage. I wish all governments were this thoroughly disorganized. If automobile companies and light bulb manufacturers were set up the way the American system of government is, we'd all still be riding horses and lighting our homes with kerosene lamps.

The anti-Federalists were responsible for the first ten amendments to the Constitution called the Bill of Rights. These further restrict the government's ability to harm us.

Let me be very clear about this. Read the Constitution yourself. Notice how complex and contorted the system is. It is a horrendously inefficient way to get things done. The people who created it obviously wanted it to perform very few services. (See Article X of the Bill of Rights, which says the government is allowed to do only those very few things specifically stated in the Constitution.) Mostly they wanted it to just sit there taking up space. This is how America became the most free and prosperous land ever known. Its government was deliberately created brain dead.

Unfortunately, nothing lasts forever. The work of the Founders, both Federalists and anti-Federalists, has largely been undone. Their work suffered a severe blow during the Civil War, and it's been gradually eroded ever since until there's not much left. America now has the most powerful government ever seen on earth.

This is probably why so few Americans know about the anti-Federalists. The arguments against creation of the Federal government have been erased from our culture. But now *you* know.

Please do yourself a favor and look into the great debate between the Federalists and anti-Federalists. It's a fine way to understand what's gone wrong in America, and it will give you some ideas about the way things ought to be.

Uncle Eric

P.S.   Chris, I think the Federalists are some of the most misunderstood people in history, especially Alexander Hamilton; he is often cited as a royalist.

I think Hamilton was a very strong juris naturalist, and he saw a monarchy as a way to get there.

We are living in an age when people have been taught that democracy and liberty are the same thing. So, anyone who opposes democracy (majority rule) is seen as anti-liberty.

In 1787, people knew the difference, and many saw majority rule as mob rule. In 1787, a person who advocated democracy was seen as a lunatic in favor of chaos (which I think is entirely accurate).

In the Federalist Papers, Hamilton made it clear he thought the state governments were mad dogs that needed to be kept on a short leash, and he was looking for a way to create that leash. He had earlier suggested monarchy, and when that idea did not fly, he turned to federalism.

I think Hamilton was a clear-eyed realist and a genius who was one of the few with the courage to face the fact that having no government was not a politically acceptable option, so if a government existed, how could it be kept under control?

Hamilton says clearly in Federalist Paper #1 that he is afraid the central government will not be strong enough to keep the democratic states from going mad. He warns about the "dangerous ambition," "jealousies and fears," "avarice, personal animosity," and "perverted ambition" in the states, and offers a plan—the Constitution—to keep these very human vices from ruining us. He worries about the "demagogues" and "tyrants" that spring up in any population.

No one admires Thomas Jefferson more than I do, but he did such an effective job of convincing us that "the people" can be trusted with power that today we see Alexander Hamilton and most other issues through the lens Jefferson created.

If truth be known, I suspect Jefferson didn't really believe it himself; he was just leaning in the direction of majority rule to keep the power junkies that surrounded the Federalist leaders from pulling these leaders too far in the direction of oligarchy.

It is crucial to remember that, once the French Revolution and Reign of Terror broke out, even the leader of the anti-Federalists, Patrick Henry, came around to seeing things Hamilton's way. This does not mean they stopped believing in liberty, it means they saw democracy for the threat to liberty that it really is.

25

Summary

Dear Chris,

Before I end this series of letter I'll give you my usual summary.

1. Political philosophies and events may seem confusing but they are easy to understand if you focus your attention not on rich vs. poor or left vs. right, but on liberty vs. political power.

2. Political power is the prize liberals, moderates, and conservatives compete for. They want it, and after they get it they want to use it on us. After all, what's the point of having power if you can't use it on someone?

3. Liberals, moderates, and conservatives are all statists. They disagree only about the specific ways power should be used.

4. Liberals want to control your economic conduct. Conservatives want to control your social conduct. Moderates are a compromise, they want to control both.

5. The non-statists are the people I call juris naturalists. The only controls they want are the two fundamental laws that make civilization possible: 1) do all you have agreed to do, and 2) do not encroach on other persons or their property.

6. The juris naturalist view is the view of the American Founders, but it has been almost forgotten. Most Americans today do not know there is an alternative to the scramble for power.

7. None of what I've written in this series of letters or anywhere else is meant to imply that liberals, moderates, or conservatives are bad people or that they have bad intentions. In most cases I honestly believe they participate in the scramble for power simply because they do not know there is another way. Since about 1945 the statist side is the only side commonly taught in the schools. Most teachers were taught only one viewpoint so this is what they teach. The system of liberty described in my previous sets of letters has been forgotten.

8. Returning to the problem of viewpoints, whenever you read anything, except math and the hard sciences (physics, chemistry, biology), you are reading an editorial. The writer slants his work by the facts he chooses to report. It's not because he's dishonest, it's because he can't report everything, so he chooses what he thinks is important, and omits the rest. Always ask, what is this writer's slant?

I'd like to see a world in which a writer always discloses his viewpoint so that readers know the model the writer used to decide what information is important and what isn't. Symbols could be used. Perhaps:

C	Conservative
F	Fascist
JN	Juris naturalist
K	Keynesian
L	Liberal
LB	Libertarian
M	Moderate
S	Socialist

Let me be the first to use such a system: Uncle Eric, JN

Some information sources have already recognized the need for disclosure. For example, WORLD PRESS REVIEW ONLINE, (www.worldpress.org) includes articles from newspapers and magazines from around the world.

In my final letter I'll explain why small encroachments are sometimes not so small.

Uncle Eric, JN

Even some of the math and hard sciences are arguable and must be considered as editorials, but the vast bulk of math and the hard sciences are proven fact. For instance, no one disputes the truth of 2 + 2 = 4, or F = Mass x Acceleration. It is worth noting that each time you ride in a car or airplane you are betting your life that the scientific principles used by the engineers who designed the vehicles were correct. We each perform so many acts of faith in science each day that we do not think about them. We notice only when something does not work. And, even then, if we flip the switch and the light does not come on, we never assume the laws of electronics have ceased to work, we assume only that a gadget somewhere has broken because this actually turns out to be the case. The tiny, leading edge parts of science may be in dispute, but the *billions* of everyday applications are not.

$$Q = \frac{-k\,A\,\Delta\,t}{\Delta\,x}$$

Heat Transfer through Conduction Formula

Equation engineers use for insulating tiles on outside of space shuttles, which is reliable enough for astronauts to risk their lives.

Are School History Books Objective?[25]

Ronald Reagan was one of the most popular presidents of the 20th century, he won two landslide elections. But when professors Robert K. Murray of Penn State and Tim H. Blessing of Alvernia College surveyed historians about Reagan's performance as president, they found the historians disagreed with the American voters. Murray and Blessing found:

- 17% of historians rated Reagan average
- 44% rated him below average
- 18% rated him a total failure

Nine out of ten historians considered Reagan intellectually unqualified to be president. Overall, they felt his social policy was "wrongheaded and malignant," reported Murray and Blessing.

For an opinion about the way historians view Reagan, the Associated Press interviewed Martin Anderson, a scholar at the Hoover Institution at Stanford University. AP reported, "Anderson said it reveals nothing but their political tilt. He said academic historians often pose as evenhanded, but are 'guided by pure political bias and bile.' "

These historians are the people who write the school history books that form the political opinions of tomorrow's leaders. Are the books objective? What do you think?

---

[25] Portions of this article were extracted from an Associated Press story that appeared in THE SACRAMENTO BEE newspaper, December 10, 1993.

26

Encroachment, Big and Small

Dear Chris,

As explained in my previous set of letters, one of the fundamental laws that make civilization possible is, do not encroach on other persons or their property. I'll end this series of letters with a few thoughts about encroachment.

We normally think of the government's encroachment in regard to large, highly visible issues, such as taxes, conscription, and the prohibition of alcohol, cocaine, etc. But encroachment may be more important in less visible areas.

For instance, when I go to bed I normally set my alarm to wake up at 7:00 a.m. One Thursday a few years ago I was rudely brought up out of a sound sleep by a trash collection truck at 5:50 a.m. The big diesel engine was roaring through the neighborhood accompanied by the clanging of trash cans and squealing of brakes.

In my town it was illegal for anyone to make loud noises before 7:00 a.m. (8:00 a.m. on weekends). I naturally assumed there must be some mistake. Perhaps the driver of the truck was new and didn't realize he should not encroach on others. I called the trash collection company and asked them to refrain from waking me up. Naive.

The supervisor told me it was their policy to start work early, and that was that, good-by.

After another half dozen phone calls I discovered the problem. The trash company had obtained a special legal privilege to work early in the mornings. They had political connections.

Our neighborhood happened to be the one where the trash company liked to begin its route, so in the dark of the early morning each Thursday the trash truck came through clanging, roaring and banging, waking everyone up.

If you or I did this, the police would be after us for disturbing the peace. But the trash company acquired the legal privilege of encroaching.

It's a small thing. Losing an hour or two of sleep one day each week is an annoyance, but it is by no means serious.

On the other hand, there's that straw that broke the camel's back.

In any neighborhood there are likely to be several business owners; some of them are likely to be experiencing difficulties in their businesses, especially in hard times. They are working twelve or fourteen hours per day trying to keep their firms alive. One serious mistake, and it's bankruptcy, dozens or hundreds of workers lose their jobs.

What happens if one of these overworked business people regularly loses an hour of precious sleep each week?

And it isn't just business owners. Many people experience hard times, it's part of life. An hour's lost sleep that would mean little when all is going well for them can be crucially important when times are tough. I'm reminded of Benjamin Franklin's thought:

For the want of a nail the shoe was lost,
For the want of a shoe the horse was lost,
For the want of a horse the rider was lost,
For the want of a rider the battle was lost,
For the want of a battle the kingdom was lost—
And all for want of a horseshoe-nail.

> —Benjamin Franklin
> *Poor Richard,* 1758

Being a man, I've never had a baby, but I know that a young mother can be in great pain while at the same time under the enormous pressure of taking care of the new baby; she often doesn't get much sleep. I can only imagine how the trash truck that's only a minor nuisance to me must sound to her when it brings her up out of a sound sleep only one hour after she was finally able to doze off.

The trash company's special permission to encroach isn't the only such privilege. Our legal system now grants this privilege to anyone who has political influence. Every day in a hundred ways we are subjected to noises, smells, poison gases, taxes, prohibitions, and restrictions that each by itself would not be serious but taken together are highly stressful. They can drive a person around the bend.

Added to this plethora of small legal encroachments are others by vandals, thieves, rapists, kidnappers, and murderers, and by friends and neighbors who just don't know any better.

In our society, fear and stress grow like a cancer, and not one person in a thousand can put his finger on exactly why— encroachment, endless encroachment, mostly in small ways.

Each time I read about an otherwise normal, decent person who has suddenly gone berserk and gunned down innocent bystanders, I wonder why it doesn't happen more often.

I'm sure the good folks at the trash company did not feel the least bit guilty about their encroachment. The law permitted them to do it.

The mainstream political viewpoints all participate in the encroachment. They want it. As we've seen in previous letters, each opposes certain types of encroachment, but each also has its own list of exceptions they believe are good and necessary.

The juris naturalist says, let's stop the encroachment, all of it. No exceptions. No special privileges. All men are created equal.

If we don't, we could end up like the former USSR, the Balkans, Caucasus, and Mideast. There, when strong central governments were in control, various groups were able to acquire political power, meaning the privilege of encroaching on others. Now that these privileged groups no longer have the protection of strong central governments, their former victims are arming themselves and getting revenge. Some of the wars have killed thousands and are likely to last for decades.

Each time in my daily life when I run into another case of encroachment, I wonder if there is someone nearby who is experiencing the same annoyance but is already near the end of his rope. This is one reason I try to be as gentle and even-tempered toward others as I can, it's for my own protection.

Chris, I know you care about what's happening to America, so I'll end with the same request as in my previous sets of letters. Please help spread the word about the need to return to the system of liberty.

Uncle Eric, JN

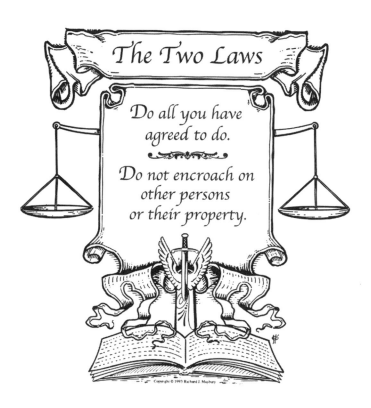

The Two Laws

Do all you have agreed to do.

Do not encroach on other persons or their property.

Spread the Word

Bibliography

- ANTI-FEDERALIST PAPERS AND THE CONSTITUTIONAL CONVENTION DEBATES edited by Ralph Ketcham, published by New American Library, a division of Penguin Putnam, NY.

- ANTI-FEDERALISTS, THE, by Jackson Turner Main, published by W.W. Norton & Co., New York.

- ADAM'S CHRONICLES by Jack Shepherd, published by Little Brown, Boston, MA.

- ANCIENT ROME: HOW IT AFFECTS YOU TODAY by Richard Maybury, published by Bluestocking Press, web site: www.BluestockingPress.com

- CATO'S LETTERS by Thomas Gordon and John Trenchard, excerpts, contained in the ENGLISH LIBERTARIAN HERITAGE, edited by David L. Jacobson, published by Fox & Wilkes, San Francisco, CA.

- COMMON SENSE AND THE DECLARATION OF INDEPENDENCE, Knowledge Products audio history, Nashville, TN.

- FEDERALIST PAPERS by Hamilton, Madison and Jay, published by New American Library, a division of Penguin Putnam, NY.

- FREE TO CHOOSE by Milton Friedman, published by Harvard University Press.

- MANZANAR by John Hershey with photographs by Ansel Adams, published by Random House. Out of print.

- MARK SKOUSEN'S COMPLETE GUIDE TO FINANCIAL PRIVACY by Mark Skousen, published by Alexandria House, Alexandria, VA.

- WASHINGTON'S FAREWELL ADDRESS, published by Applewood Books, MA.

- WHATEVER HAPPENED TO JUSTICE? by Richard J. Maybury, published by Bluestocking Press, web site: www.BluestockingPress.com

Book Suppliers

- Advocates for Self-Government, Inc., phone: 800-932-1776, web site: www.self-gov.org

- Bluestocking Press, phone: 800-959-8586, web site: www.BluestockingPress.com

- Foundation for Economic Education, phone: 800-960-4FEE, web site: www.fee.org

- Laissez Faire Books, phone, 800-326-0996, web site: LFB.com

- Liberty Tree Network, phone: 800-927-8733, web site: www.liberty-tree.org

Contact your librarian or a used bookstore for locating out-of-print books.

Glossary

ANARCHISM. Originally, advocating no political government. Now often used to mean advocating terrorism.

ANARCHIST. Originally, one who does not believe in political government. Now, often used to mean a terrorist.

AUSTRIAN ECONOMICS. The most free-market of all the economic viewpoints today. The origin was in Vienna, Austria, but the country where it is most popular today is probably the U.S. Austrian economists have won Nobel Prizes, and the most widely known Austrian economist, F.H. Hayek, was highly influential in the economic policies of British Prime Minister Margaret Thatcher.

BOLSHEVIK. Originally, a member of the Social Democratic Party of Russia around 1917. Now, any socialist or communist.

CAPITALIST. One who believes in capitalism.

CAPITALISM. A term coined by Socialist Karl Marx, who meant the stage of economic development in which large amounts of capital (tools) are accumulated by private firms. Today capitalism is generally taken to mean free markets, free trade, and free enterprise. The economic philosophy of the right.

CENTRIST. Moderate.

CIVIL LIBERTARIAN. One who believes strongly in the need to protect the individual's rights to free speech, press, religion, assembly, and privacy, but usually not property.

CLASSICAL LIBERAL. Juris naturalist. One who believes that the country should have a small, weak government, and free markets, and that the individual is endowed by his Creator with inalienable rights to his life, liberty, and property. Also, one who believes in Natural Law and common law, or Higher Law.

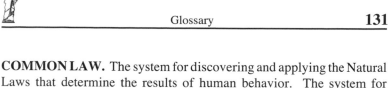

COMMON LAW. The system for discovering and applying the Natural Laws that determine the results of human behavior. The system for discovering and applying the Natural Laws that govern the human ecology. The body of definitions and precedents growing from the two fundamental laws that make civilization possible: (1) do all you have agreed to do, and (2) do not encroach on other persons or their property.

COMMUNIST. Originally, a socialist who is striving for the utopia of communism in which there is no government and all live according to the rule, "from each according to his ability, to each according to his needs." Now, one who believes in a dictatorial government that owns and controls everything and everyone.

CONSERVATIVE. A person on the right side of the left-right political spectrum. Conservatives believe in economic freedom and social control.

CONTRACT LAW. Law of agreements.

COUNTRY. A geographic area controlled by a government.

CRIME. Anything a government punishes.

CRIMINAL LAW. Laws enacted by governments. Criminal law is usually taken to mean laws against violence, fraud and theft, but in actual fact, governments tend to criminalize anything they don't like.

DEMOCRAT. A member of the Democratic Party. Also, a person on the left side of the political spectrum.

EDITORIAL. A statement of opinion.

EMPOWER. To have power or to be granted power.

ENCROACH. To intrude on, or damage, the life, liberty, or property of someone who has not harmed anyone. To trespass.

EXTREMIST. One who is highly committed to a cause with which the writer or speaker does not agree.

FANATIC. Same as extremist.

FASCISM. The political philosophy that is no philosophy at all, do whatever appears necessary. Derived from the law of the Roman Empire.

FASCIST. One who believes there is no real truth. The true fascist believes that concepts such as justice and right and wrong are entirely matters of opinion. Fascists are nationalists who believe in strong central government that controls everyone according to the rule, "do whatever appears necessary." Often fascists are intolerant of minorities.

FREEDOM. Permission to do as you please.

GOVERNMENT. An organization with the legal privilege of encroaching on persons who have not harmed anyone.

GREEN PARTY. Committed to environmentalism and socialism.

HARD SCIENCE. A science in which facts are mathematically measurable and provable through experimentation and observation. Examples: Physics, chemistry, biology, astronomy.

HIGHER LAW. A law higher than any human law.

HOUSE OF COMMONS. The lower house of the British parliament. Like the House of Representatives in the U.S.

IMMORALITY. Concerns damage to yourself and perhaps to others. Immorality isn't always serious enough to warrant intervention by the heavy hand of the law.

INFLUENCE. Persuasion. Implies the ability to say no without being punished.

JURIS NATURALIS. Natural Law.

JURIS NATURALISM. The belief that there is a Natural Law that determines the results of human conduct and this law is higher than any government's law.

JURIS NATURALIST. syn. Classical liberal. Believes in Higher Law or Natural Law, that right and wrong are not matters of opinion. Believes political power corrupts both morals and judgment. Wants a government that is small and growing smaller.

KEYNESIANISM. Originally the economic philosophy of economist John Maynard Keynes. Today a kind of compromise, or middle road, between socialism and capitalism. Wants broad government controls on economic activity, especially manipulation of the money supply. "Keynesian" is sometimes used as a synonym for "inflationist," or one who advocates inflating the money supply.

LAISSEZ FAIRE. From the French, Laissez nous faire, meaning leave us alone. Says the benefits of government's economic controls are less than the total costs. Government should do nothing in the economy except enforce contracts and protect against violence and theft.

LAW. Broadly speaking, the rules for human conduct which are enforced by violence or threats of violence. More narrowly, law sometimes means common law or Natural Law, as distinct from legislation. "A nation of laws and not of men" means a nation in which the highest law is common law or Natural Law not legislation.

LEFT. The liberal side of the political spectrum.

LIBERAL. A person on the left side of the left-right political spectrum. Liberals believe in social freedom and economic control.

LIBERALISM. The philosophy of the left. Borrows much from socialism. Believes in economic statism, freedom in most non-economic matters, and less militarism.

LIBERTARIAN. Classical liberal.

LIBERTY. Protection of the individual's rights to his or her life, liberty, and property. Widespread obedience to the two fundamental laws that make civilization possible: (1) do all you have agreed to do, and (2) do not encroach on other persons or their property. Liberty is not the same as freedom.

MANNERS. Polite behavior. Courteous deportment.

MARXISM. The theory of Karl Marx that human society develops through stages ending in a utopia called communism. The belief that a dictatorial government owning and controlling everything and everyone (socialism) is a necessary step on the road to communism.

MARXIST. One who believes in the economic philosophy of Karl Marx. A socialist or communist.

MODERATE. One who is in the middle of the left-right political spectrum. Moderates advocate both economic encroachment and social encroachment, but perhaps not to the extremes that left and right do.

MONETARISM. A free-market economic philosophy. Focuses on increases in money supply causing rising prices. Associated with the economics department of the University of Chicago; monetarism is sometimes called the Chicago school of economics.

MONETARIST. One who believes in monetarism.

NATIONALIST. An extremely patriotic person who regards his nation as being of supreme importance.

NATIONALIZE. Taken over by the government.

NATURAL LAW. The rules that govern the operation of the universe and everything and everyone in it. Natural Law sometimes appears capitalized in the same way as the Ten Commandments.

NAZI. A member of the National Socialist German Workers Party. A German fascist.

POLITICAL POWER. The legal privilege of encroaching on the life, liberty or property of a person who has not harmed anyone.

POLITICIZE. To make political. To be entangled in the struggle for political power. To be under the government's control.

POPULIST. One who is not a democrat or republican but claims to be popular with rank and file voters.

RADICAL. Same as extremist.

REPUBLICAN. Conservative.

RIGHT. The conservative side of the political spectrum.

SERFDOM. Economic slavery developed through heavy taxation.

SOCIALISM. An economic and political system under which virtually everything and everyone is owned and controlled by government agencies. Marxism.

SOCIALIST. A person who advocates socialism. Most socialists have good intentions, they assume government agencies will act in the best interests of the governed, not in the best interests of the government. A Marxist.

SOCIALIZED. Owned and controlled by government.

SOFT SCIENCE. A science in which mathematically measurable and provable facts are rare. Examples: economics, sociology, psychology.

STATE. Government. Also sometimes means the combination of the government and the country as a single entity.

STATISM. The opposite of the original American philosophy. Says political power is a good thing. Government is our friend, our protector, the solution to our problems, and there is no law higher than the government's law.

STATIST. One who believes in government as the solution to problems. Statists assume the benefits of government activities can be greater than total costs.

TERRORISM. The creation of terror, usually through violence or threats of violence. As commonly used, automatically assumes the terrorist is acting without good cause.

TERRORIST. One who creates terror, usually through violence or threats of violence.

TORT. Harm done to another. Encroachment on the life, liberty, or property of a person who has not harmed anyone.

TORT LAW. The branch of common law dealing with harm one person does to another.

WARLORD. Originally, a high ranking military officer in charge of a medieval kingdom's military operations. Now an enemy military leader.

WEALTH. Goods and services. Not to be confused with money. Money can be wealth, but it is only one kind.

WELFARE STATISM. The belief that government should ensure a minimum standard of living for all, including but not necessarily limited to food, clothing, shelter, medical care, and schooling. Necessarily requires heavy taxes and a large bureaucracy to finance and administer the welfare programs. Probably the most popular leftist economic philosophy.

About Richard J. Maybury

Richard Maybury, also known as Uncle Eric, is a world renowned author, lecturer and geopolitical analyst. He consults with business firms in the U.S. and Europe. Richard is the former Global Affairs editor of MONEYWORLD and widely regarded as one of the finest free-market writers in America. Mr. Maybury's articles have appeared in THE WALL STREET JOURNAL, USA TODAY, and other major publications.

Richard Maybury has penned eleven books in the Uncle Eric series. His books have been endorsed by top business leaders including former U.S. Treasury Secretary William Simon, and he has been interviewed on more than 250 radio and TV shows across America.

He has been married for more than 35 years, has lived abroad, traveled around the world, and visited 48 states and 40 countries.

He is truly a teacher for all ages.

Index

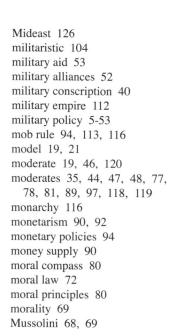

Published by Bluestocking Press

Uncle Eric Books by Richard J. Maybury

UNCLE ERIC TALKS ABOUT PERSONAL, CAREER, & FINANCIAL SECURITY
WHATEVER HAPPENED TO PENNY CANDY?
WHATEVER HAPPENED TO JUSTICE?
ARE YOU LIBERAL? CONSERVATIVE? OR CONFUSED?
ANCIENT ROME: HOW IT AFFECTS YOU TODAY
EVALUATING BOOKS: WHAT WOULD THOMAS JEFFERSON THINK ABOUT THIS?
THE MONEY MYSTERY
THE CLIPPER SHIP STRATEGY
THE THOUSAND YEAR WAR IN THE MIDEAST
WORLD WAR I: THE REST OF THE STORY
WORLD WAR II: THE REST OF THE STORY

Bluestocking Guides (study guides for the Uncle Eric books)
by Jane A. Williams and/or Kathryn Daniels

Each Study Guide includes some or all of the following:
1) chapter-by-chapter comprehension questions and answers
2) application questions and answers
3) research activities
4) essay assignments
5) thought questions
6) final exam

More Bluestocking Press Titles

LAURA INGALLS WILDER AND ROSE WILDER LANE HISTORICAL TIMETABLE
CAPITALISM FOR KIDS: GROWING UP TO BE YOUR OWN BOSS by Karl Hess
ECONOMICS: A FREE MARKET READER edited by Jane Williams & Kathryn Daniels
BUSINESS: IT'S ALL ABOUT COMMON SENSE by Kathryn Daniels & Anthony Joseph

The Bluestocking Press Catalog

Varied and interesting selections of history products: historical toys and crafts, historical documents, historical fiction, primary sources, and more.

Order information: Order any of the above by phone or online from:

Bluestocking Press
Phone: 800-959-8586
email: CustomerService@BluestockingPress.com
web site: www.BluestockingPress.com